FOR ORGANS, PIANOS & ELECTRONIC KEYBOARDS

E-Z PLAY TODAY

69

2ND EDITION

IT'S GOSPEL

T0044798

ISBN: 978-0-7935-0539-5

HAL•LEONARD®
CORPORATION
7777 W. BLUEMOUND RD. P.O. BOX 13819 MILWAUKEE, WI 53213

E-Z Play® Today Music Notation © 1975 by HAL LEONARD CORPORATION

E-Z PLAY and EASY ELECTRONIC KEYBOARD MUSIC are registered trademarks of HAL LEONARD CORPORATION.

Visit Hal Leonard Online at
www.halleonard.com

Blessed Jesus

Registration 3
Rhythm: Waltz

Words by Gloria Gaither
Music by William J. Gaither

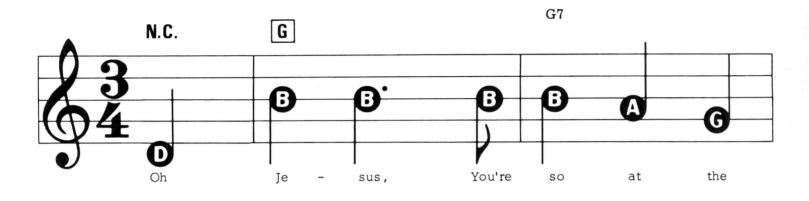

Oh Je - sus, You're so at the

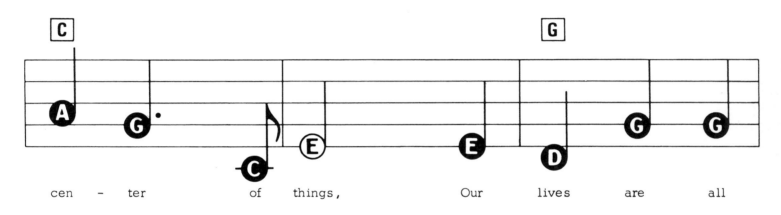

cen - ter of things, Our lives are all

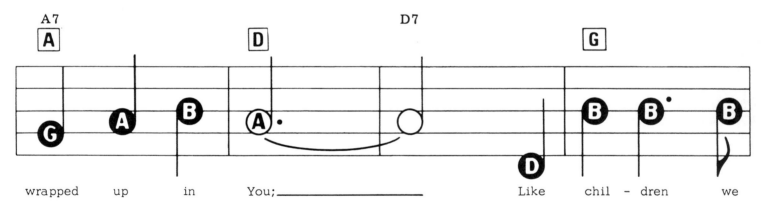

wrapped up in You;_____ Like chil - dren we

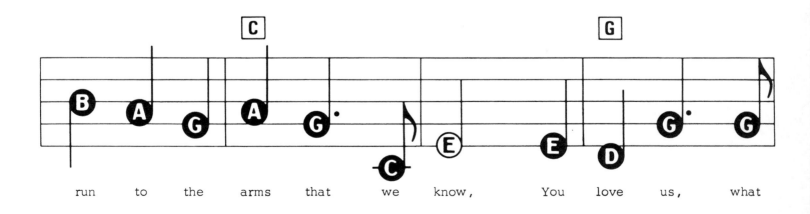

run to the arms that we know, You love us, what

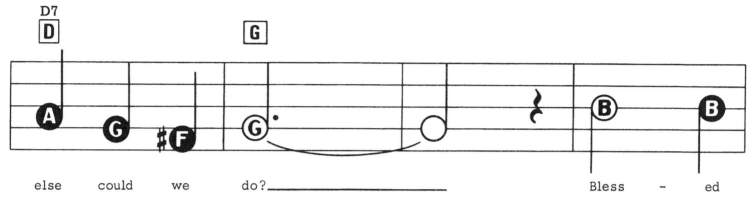

else could we do?_____ Bless – ed

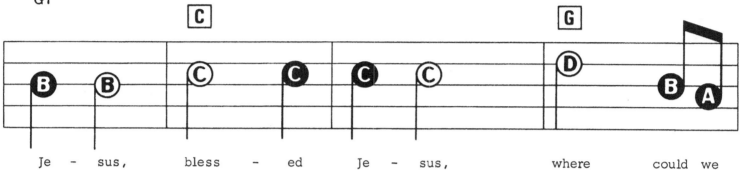

Je – sus, bless – ed Je – sus, where could we

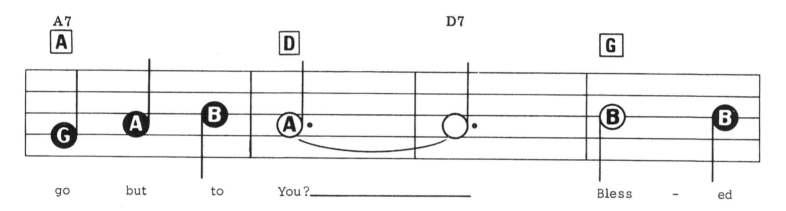

go but to You?_____ Bless – ed

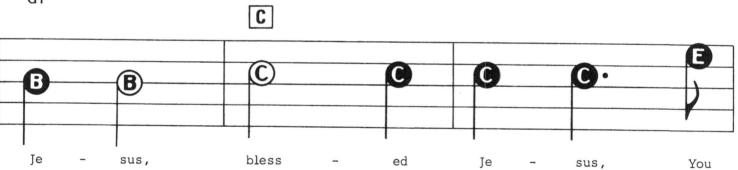

Je – sus, bless – ed Je – sus, You

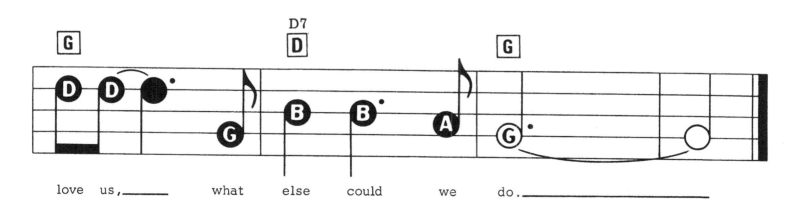

love us,_____ what else could we do._____

The Blood Will Never Lose Its Power

Registration 1
Rhythm: Waltz

Words and Music by
Andraé Crouch

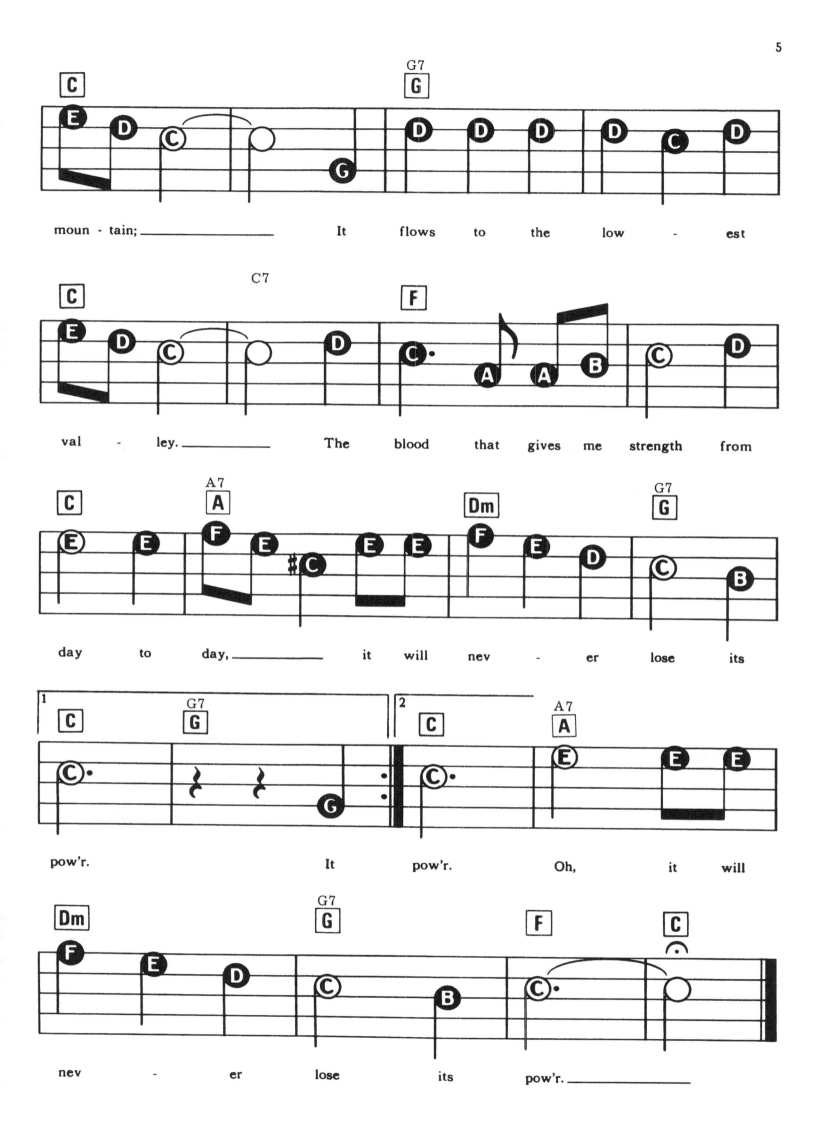

Daddy Sang Bass

Registration 5
Rhythm: Swing

Words and Music by
Carl Perkins

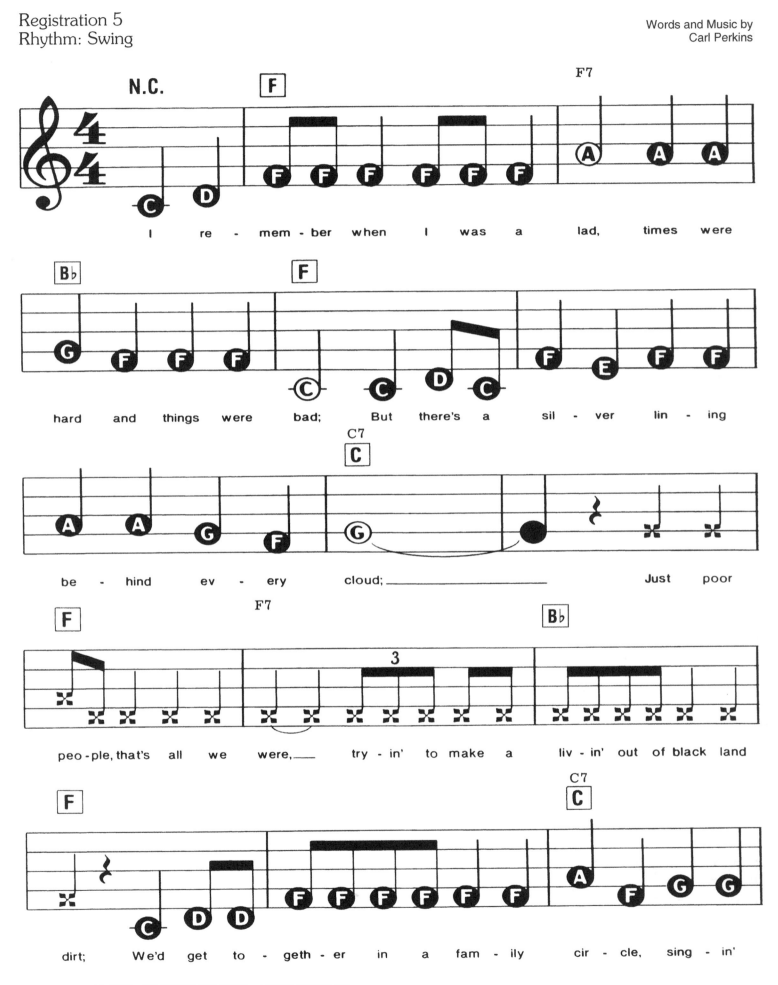

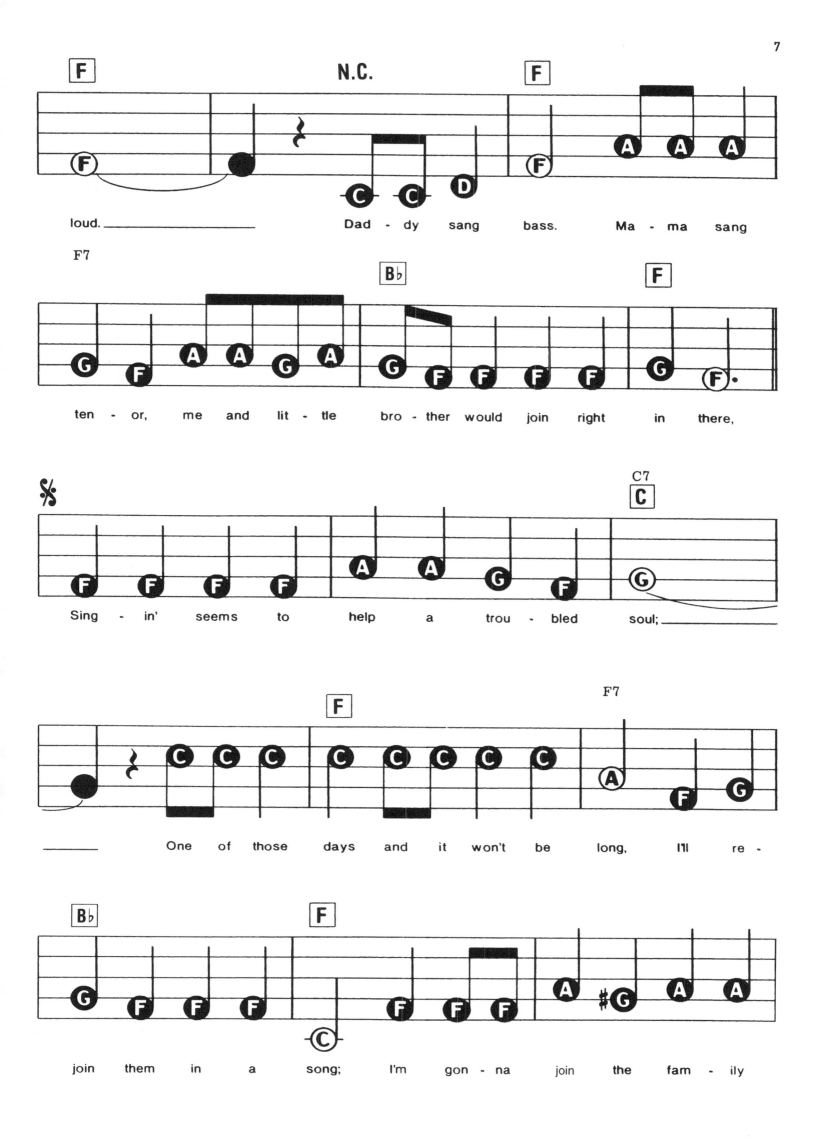

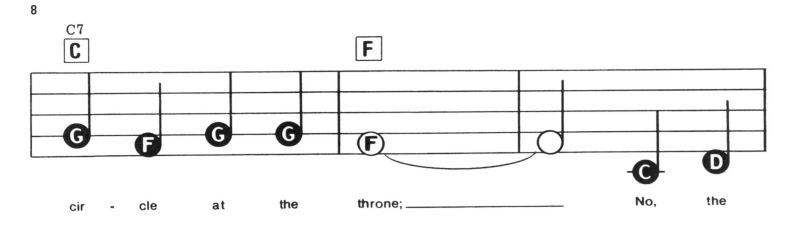

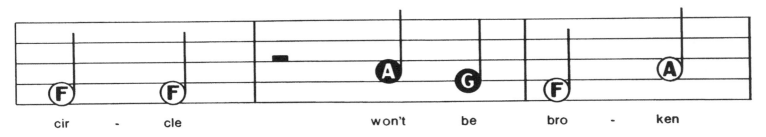

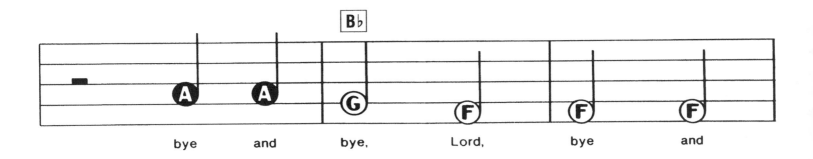

I Believe

Registration 2
Rhythm: Ballad or Slow Rock

Words and Music by Ervin Drake,
Irvin Graham, Jimmy Shirl and Al Stillman

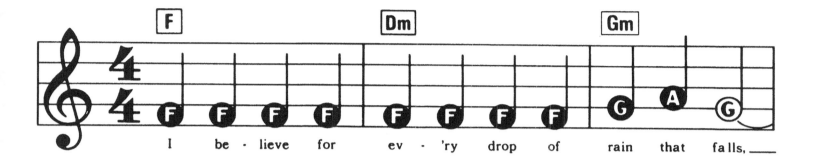

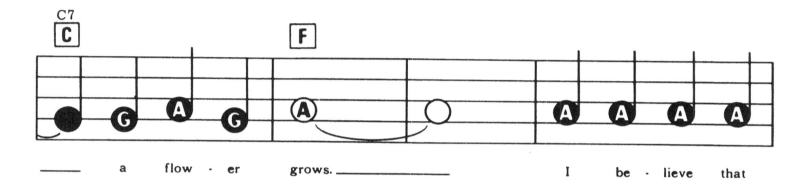

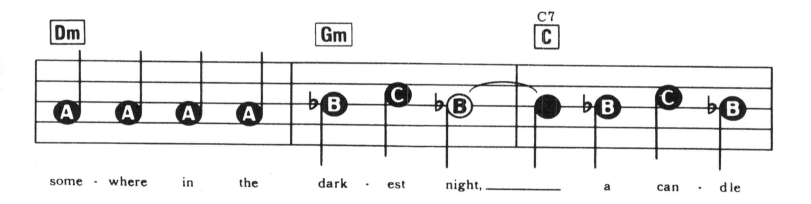

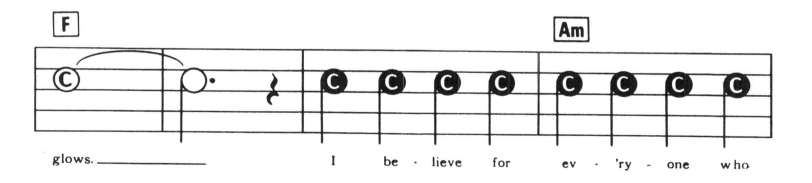

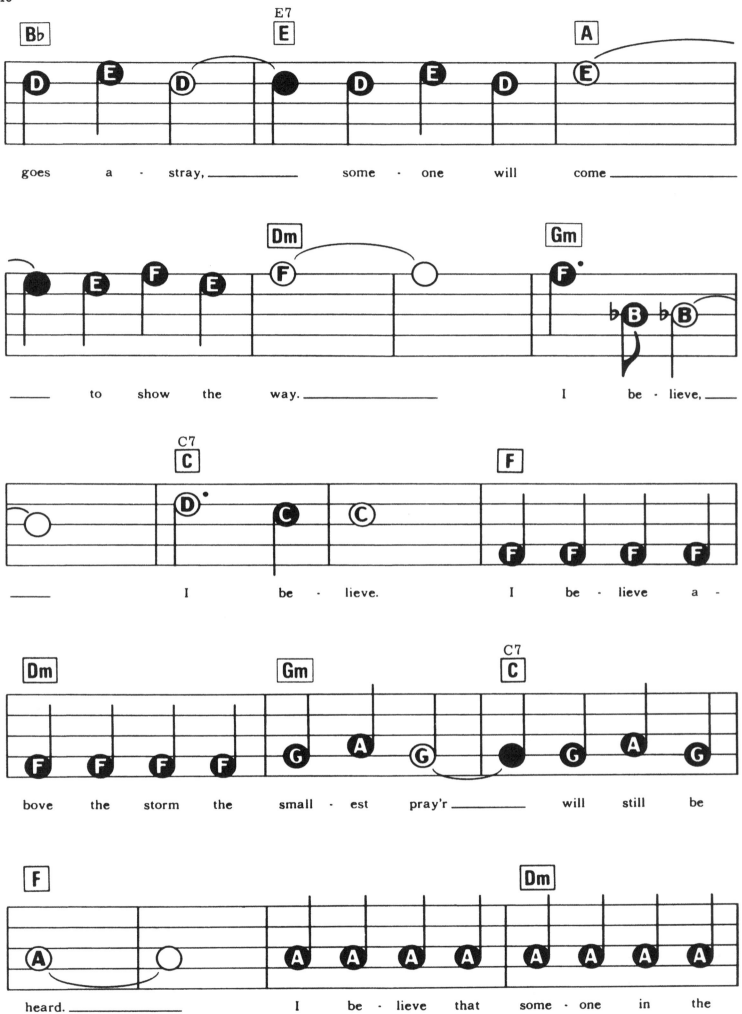

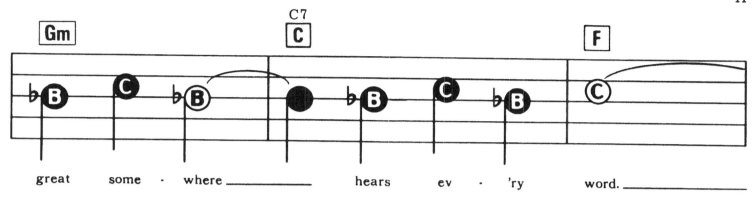

great some · where _____ hears ev · 'ry word. _____

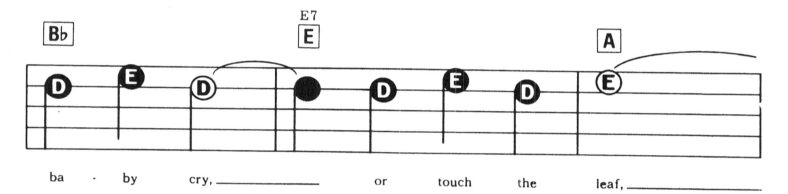

_____ Ev · 'ry time I hear a new · born

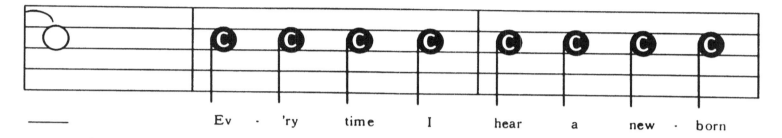

ba · by cry, _____ or touch the leaf, _____

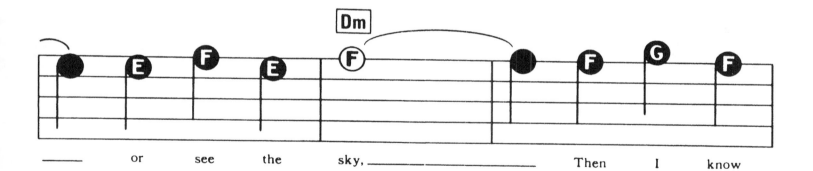

_____ or see the sky, _____ Then I know

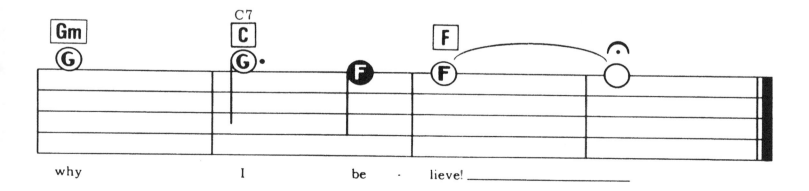

why I be · lieve! _____

His Name Is Wonderful

Registration 1
Rhythm: Waltz

Words and Music by
Audrey Mieir

His name is Won - der - ful, His name is

Won - der - ful, His name is Won - der - ful,

Je - sus, my Lord. He is the might - y King

Mas - ter of ev - 'ry - thing; His name is

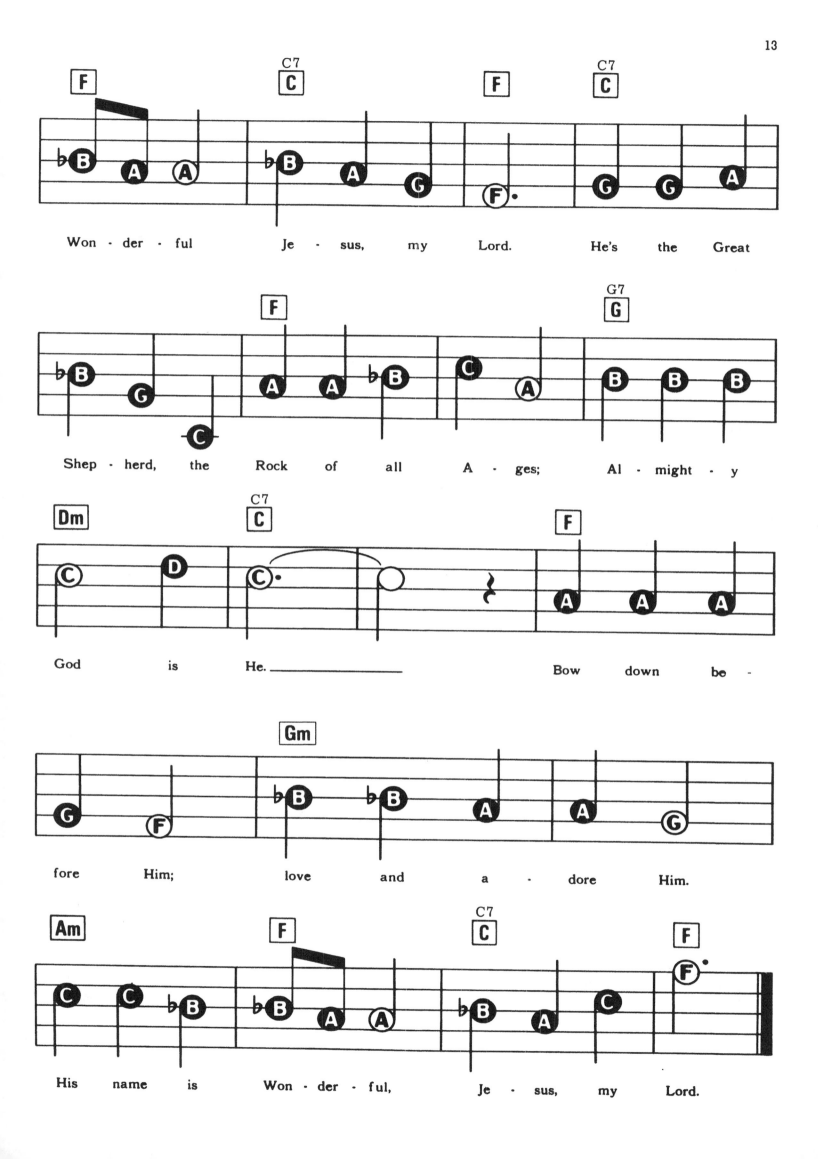

How Great Thou Art

Registration 6
Rhythm: None

Words and Music by
Stuart K. Hine

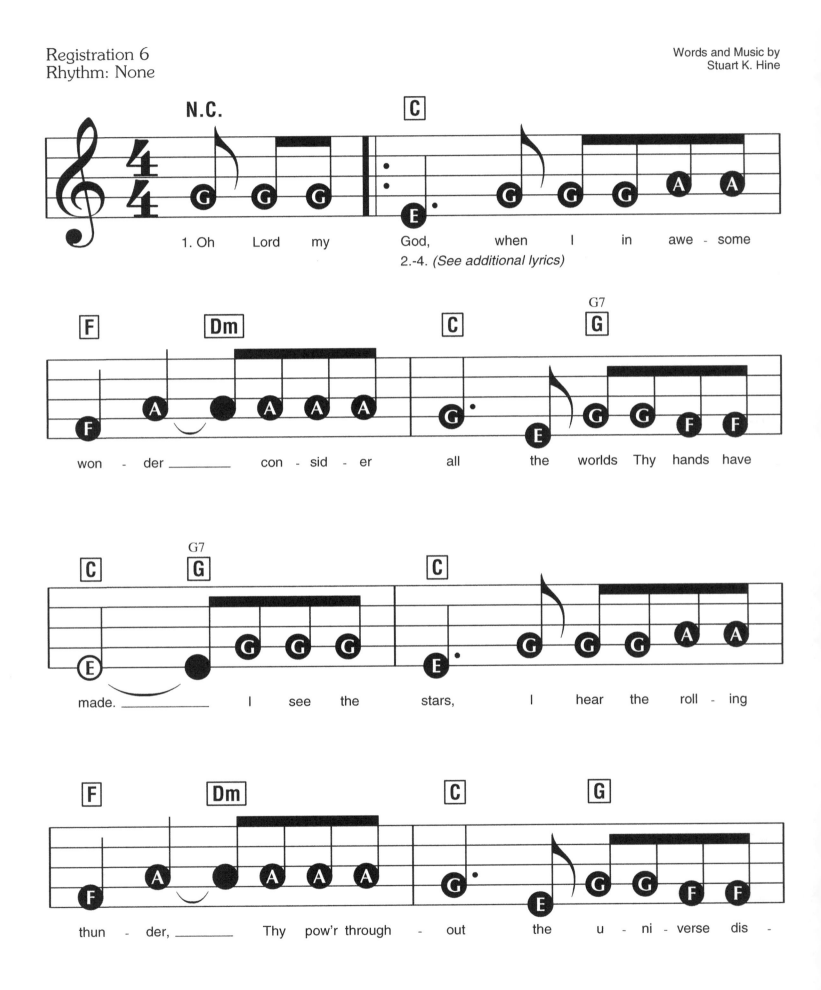

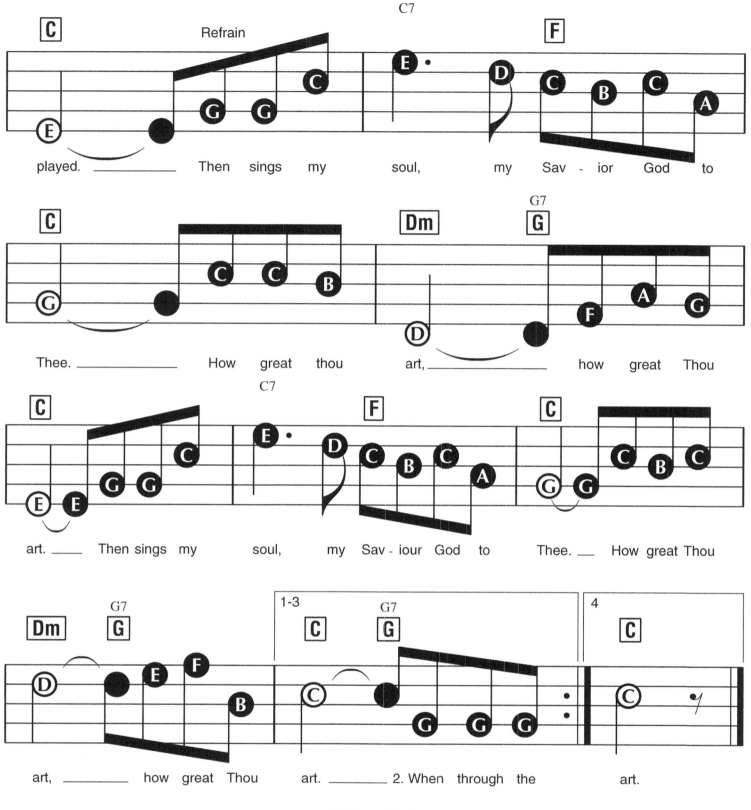

Additional Lyrics

2. When through the woods and forest glades I wander,
   And hear the birds sing sweetly in the trees.
   When I look down from lofty mountain grandeur,
   And hear the brook and feel the gentle breeze.

   Refrain

3. And when I think that God His Son not sparing,
   Sent Him to die, I scarce can take it in.
   That on the cross, my burden gladly bearing,
   He bled and died to take away my sin.

   Refrain

4. When Christ shall come with shout of acclamation
   And take me home, what joy shall fill my heart!
   Then I shall bow in humble adoration
   And there proclaim my God how great Thou art

   Refrain

I Want to Be More Like Jesus

Registration 4
Rhythm: Swing or Shuffle

Words and Music by
Thomas A. Dorsey

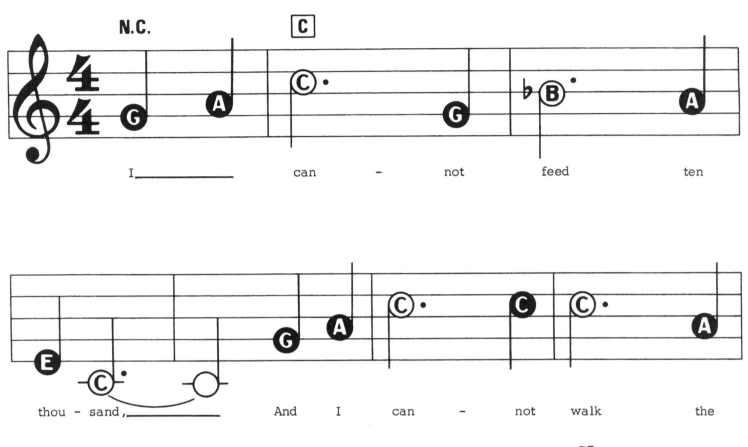

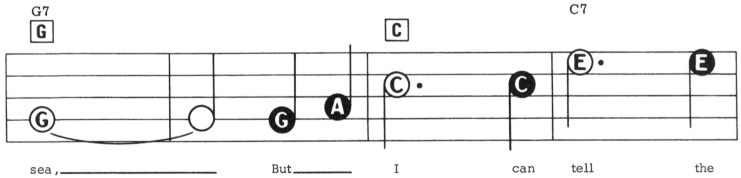

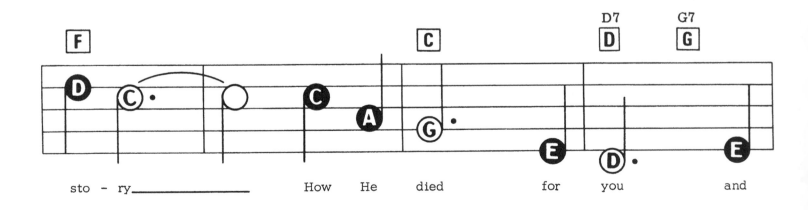

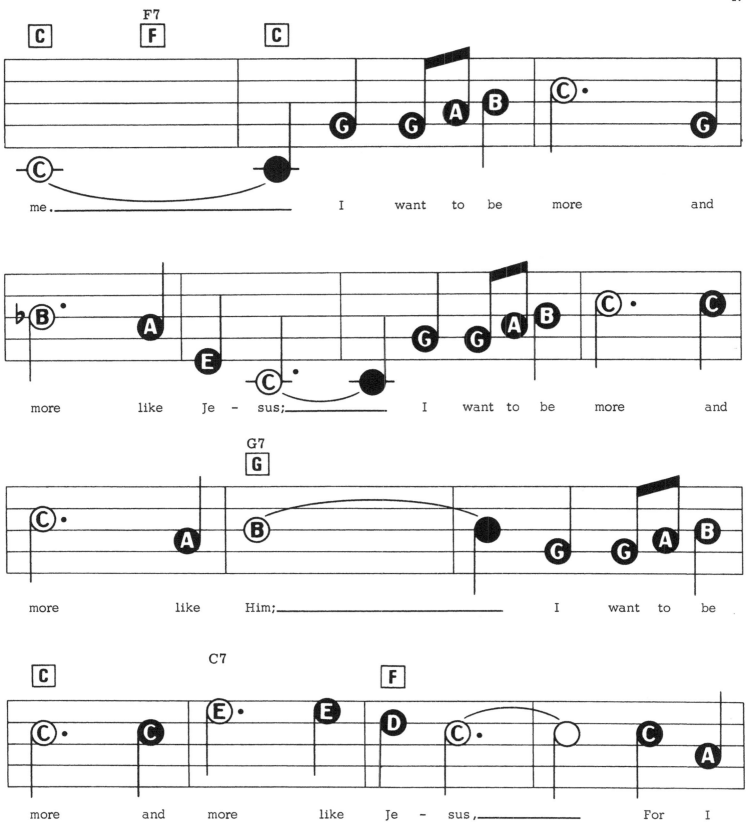

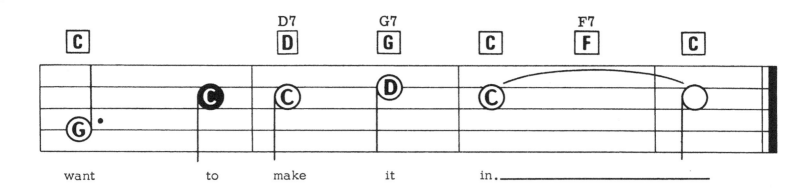

I Will Serve Thee

Registration 3
Rhythm: Swing or 8 Beat

Words by William J. and Gloria Gaither
Music by William J. Gaither

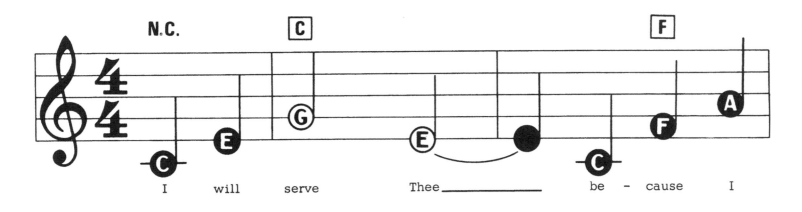

I will serve Thee _____ be - cause I

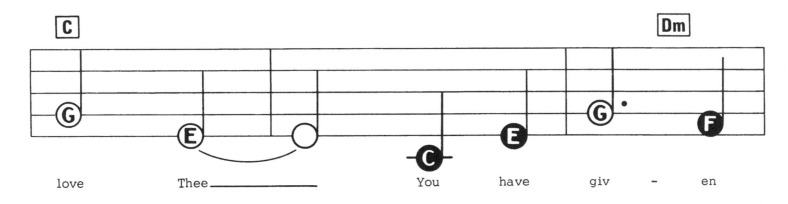

love Thee _____ You have giv - en

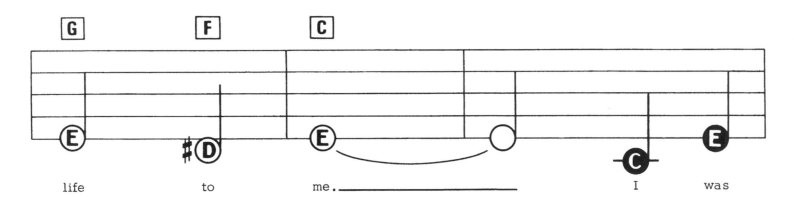

life to me. _____ I was

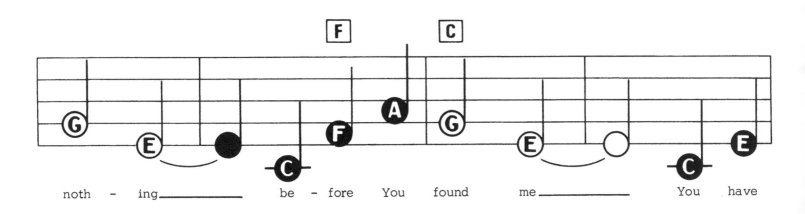

noth - ing _____ be - fore You found me _____ You have

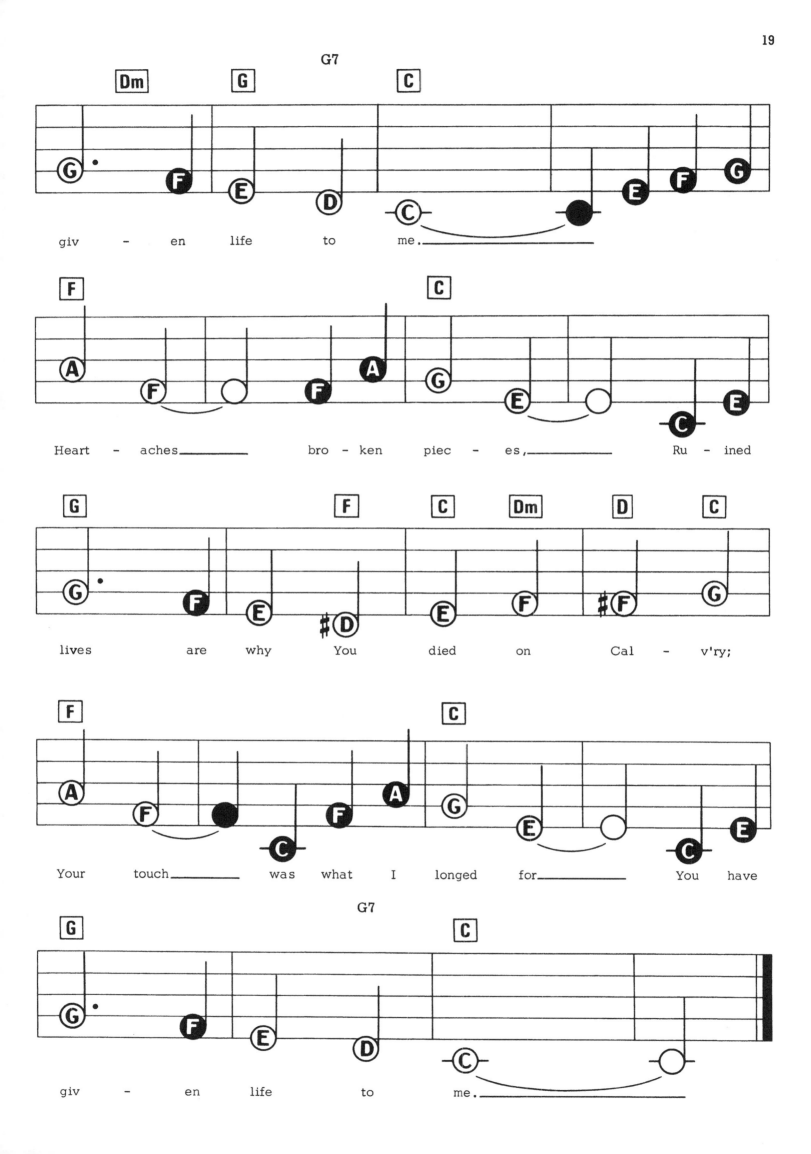

Invisible Hands

Registration 9
Rhythm: Waltz

Words and Music by Francis Stanton,
Buddy Kaye, Frederick Patrick and William Harrington

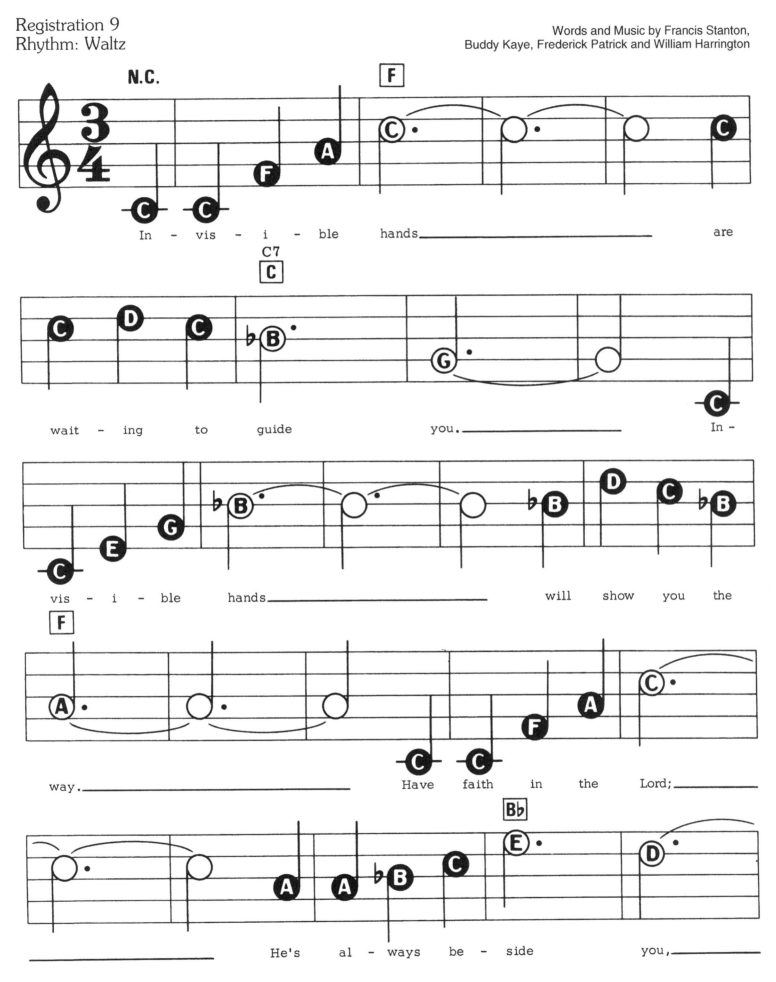

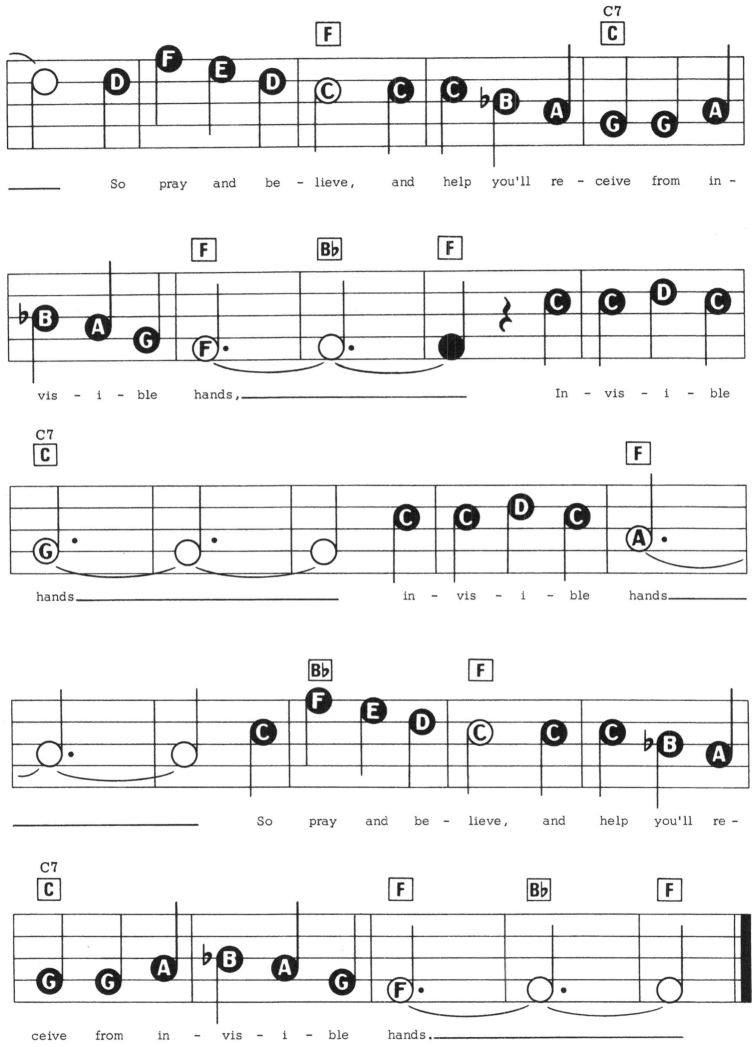

It Is No Secret
(What God Can Do)

Registration 6
Rhythm: March

Words and Music by
Stuart Hamblen

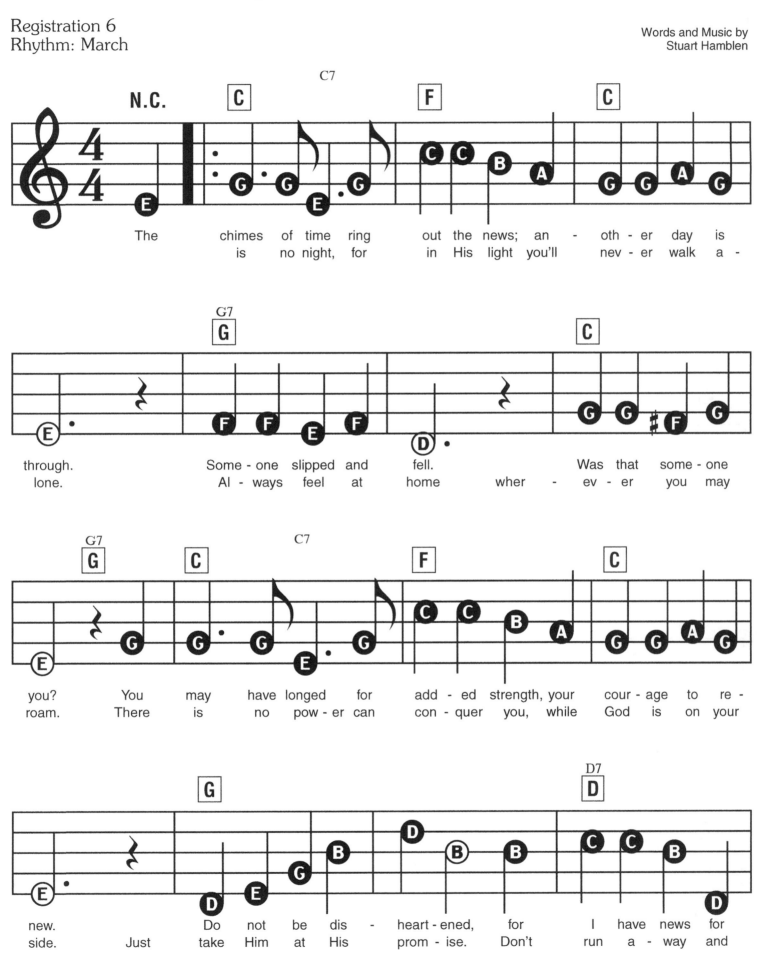

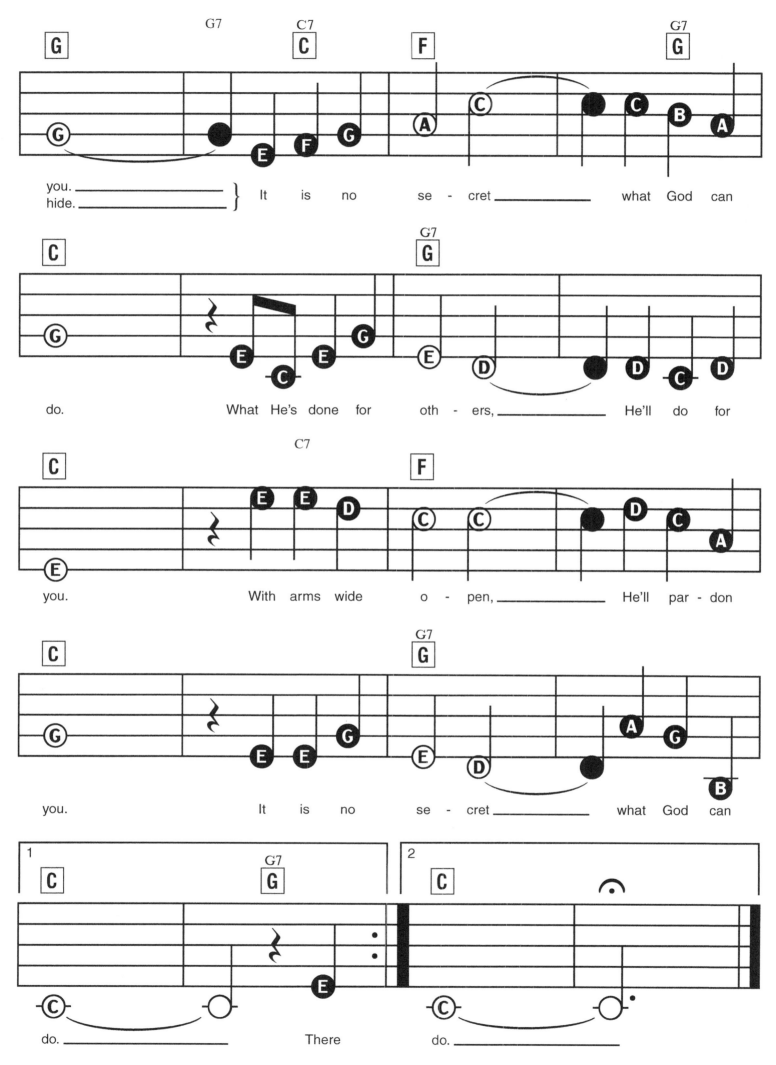

It Took a Miracle

Registration 3
Rhythm: 8 Beat or Rock

Words and Music by
John W. Peterson

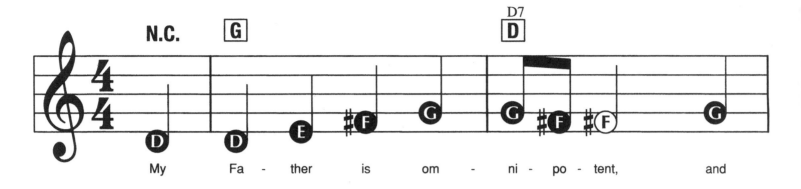

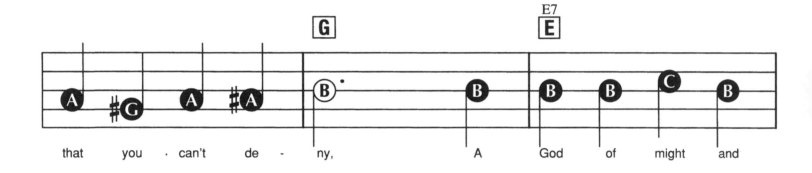

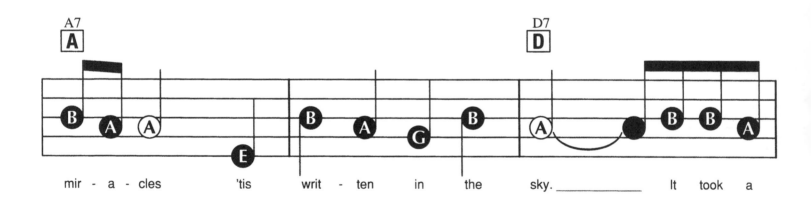

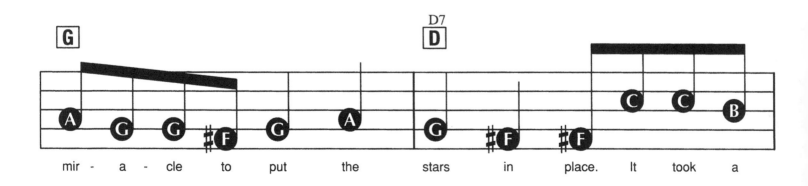

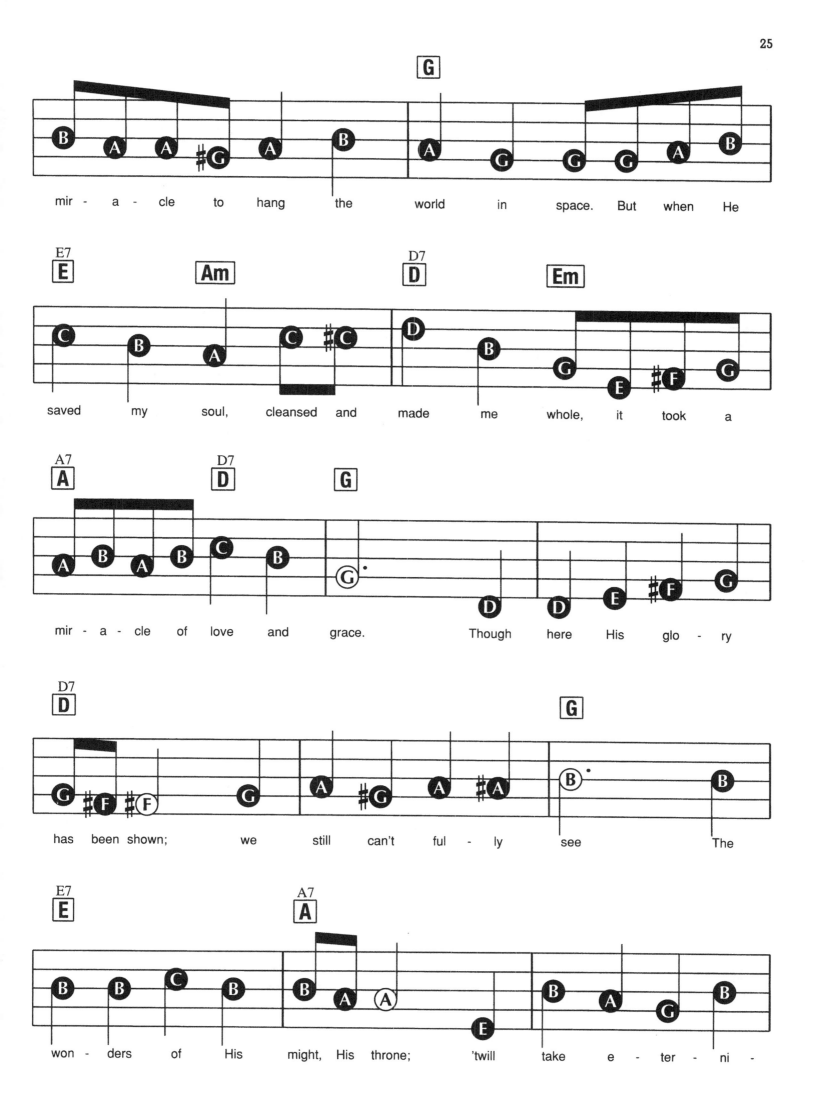

26

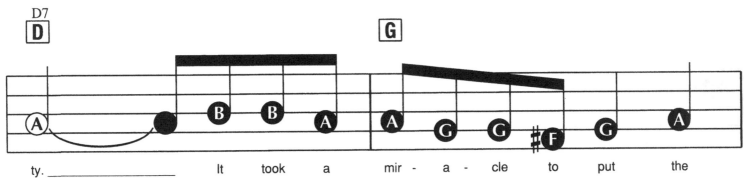

ty. _____ It took a mir - a - cle to put the

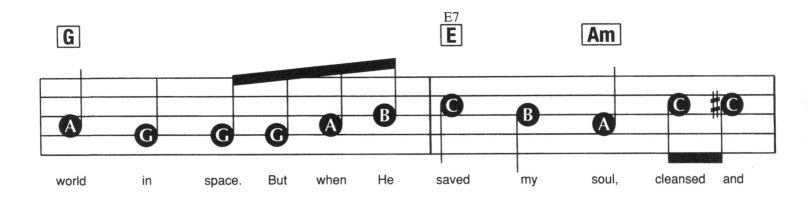

stars in place. It took a mir - a - cle to hang the

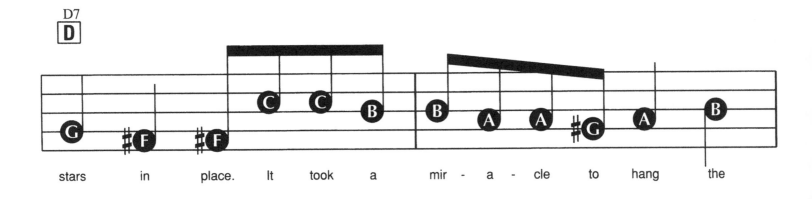

world in space. But when He saved my soul, cleansed and

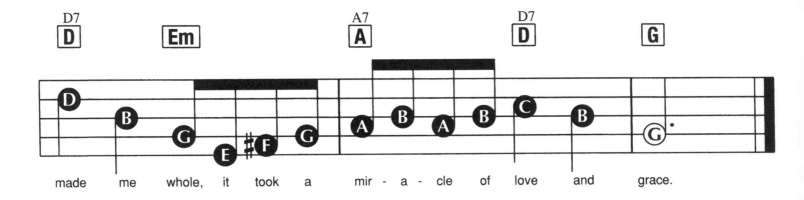

made me whole, it took a mir - a - cle of love and grace.

My God Is Real
(Yes, God Is Real)

Registration 9
Rhythm: Slow Rock or Shuffle

Words and Music by
Kenneth Morris

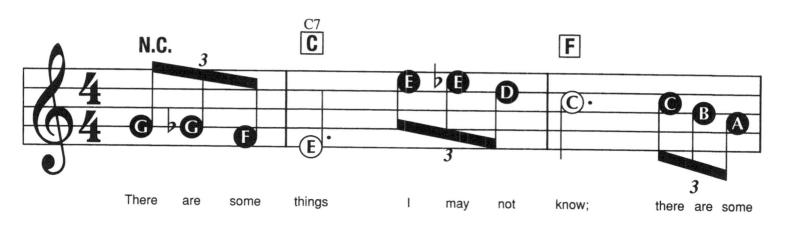

There are some things I may not know; there are some

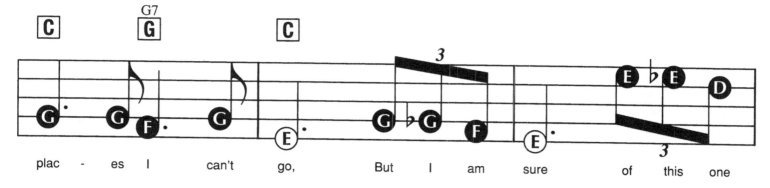

plac - es I can't go, But I am sure of this one

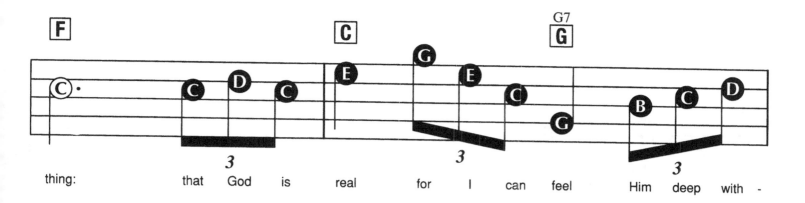

thing: that God is real for I can feel Him deep with -

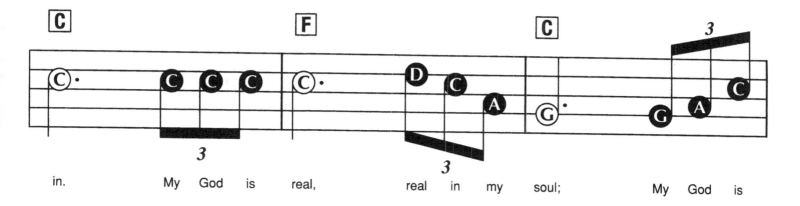

in. My God is real, real in my soul; My God is

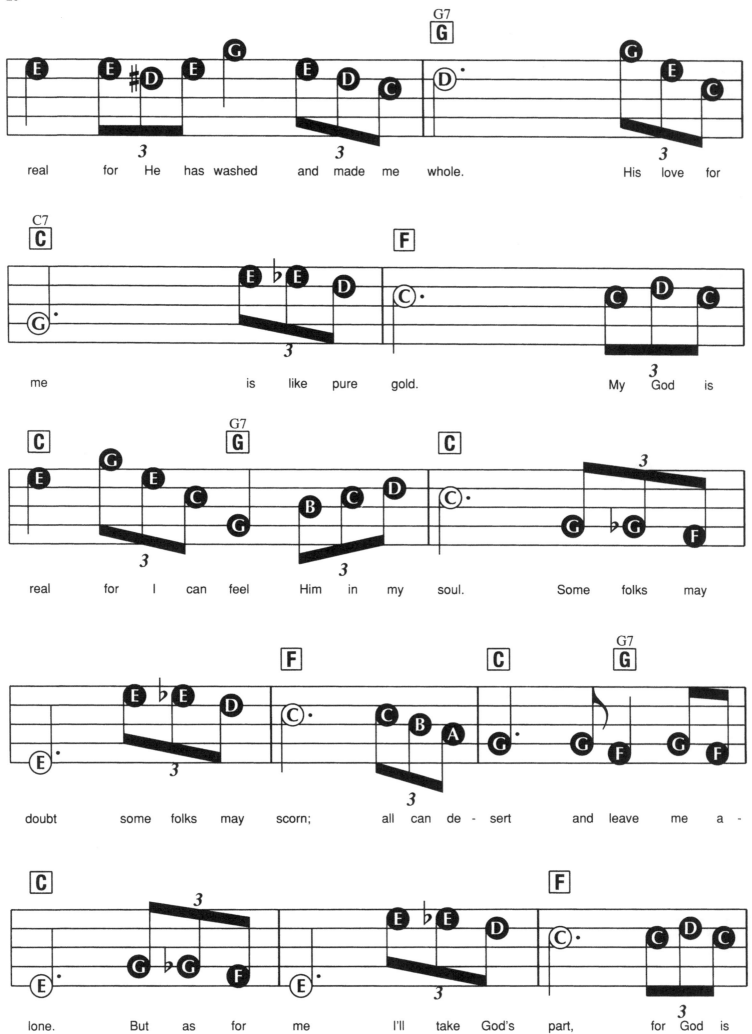

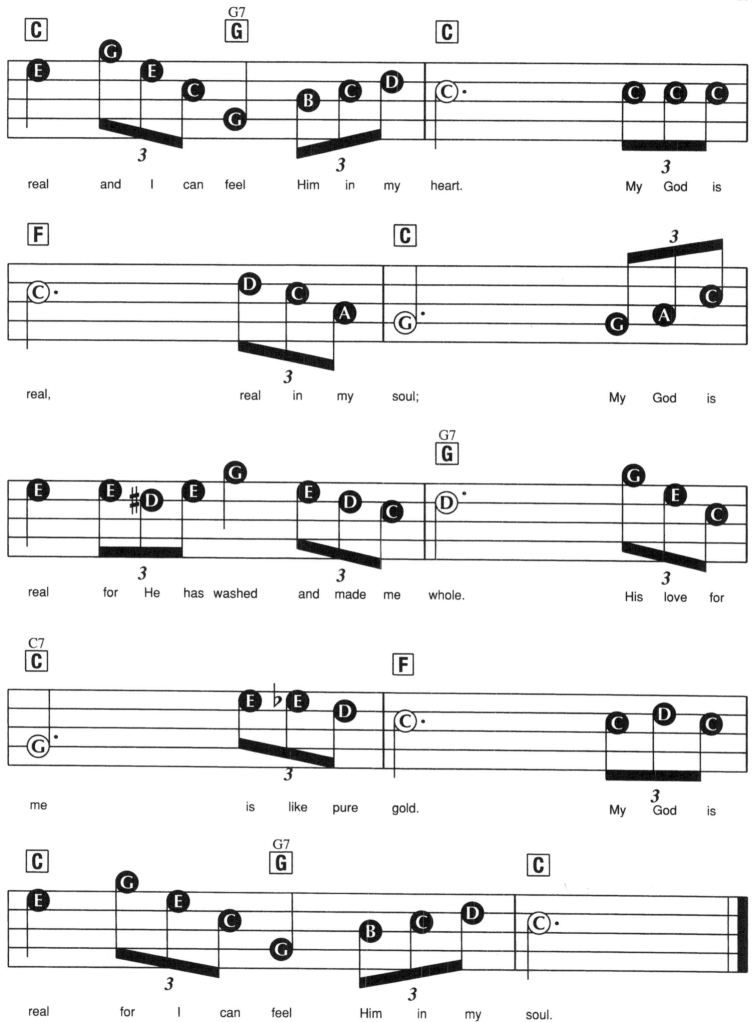

Mansion Over the Hilltop

Registration 5
Rhythm: Swing

Words and Music by
Ira F. Stanphill

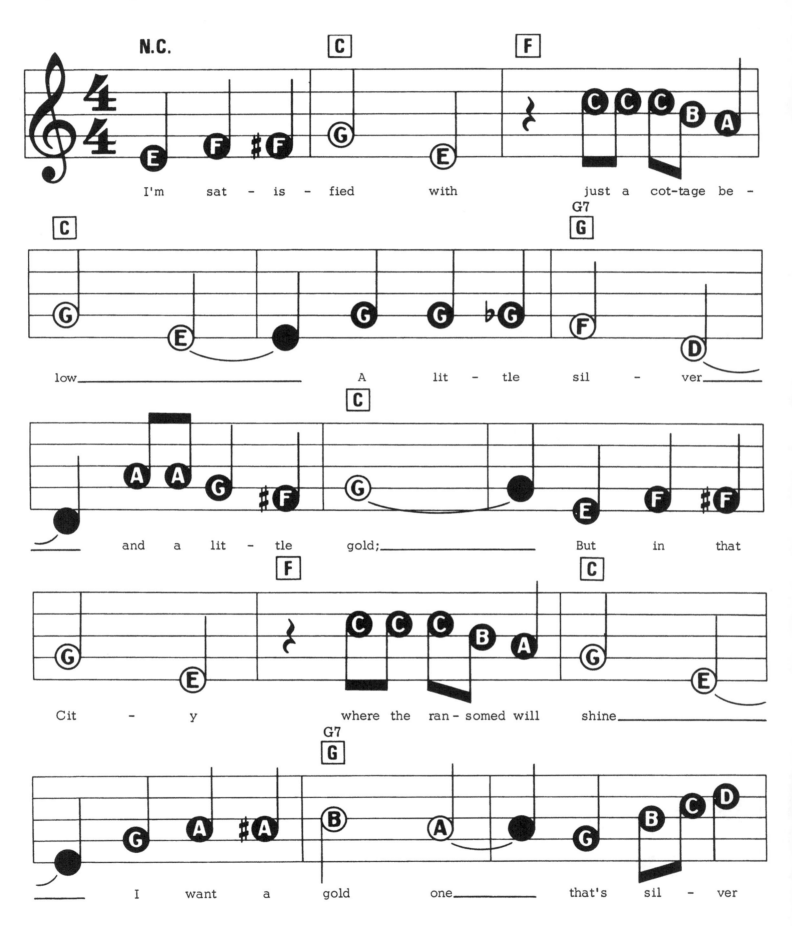

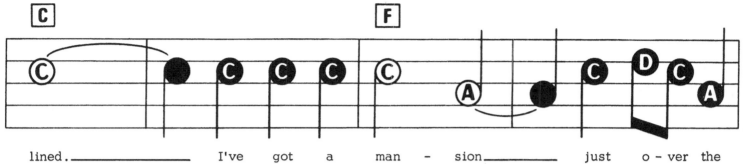

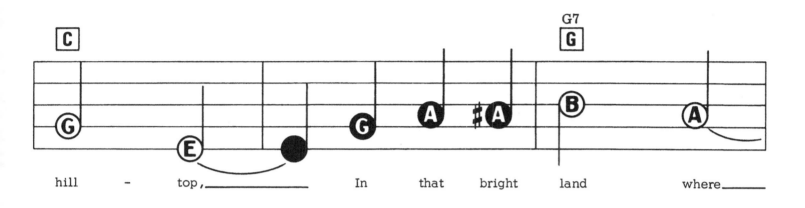

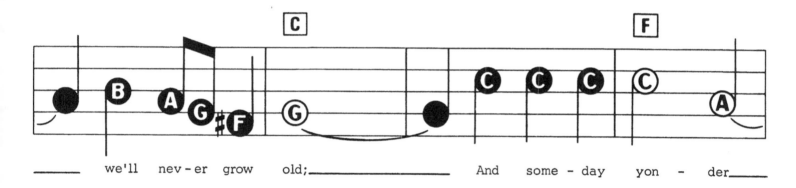

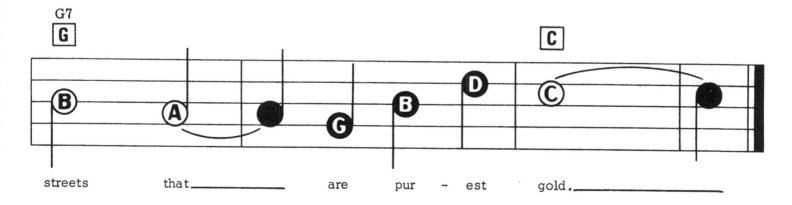

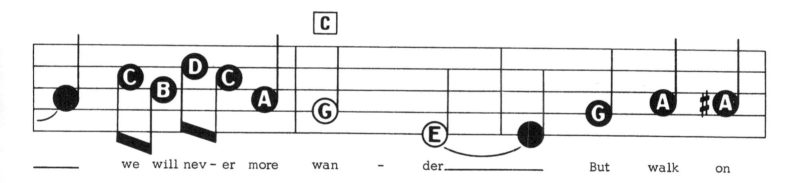

My Tribute

Registration 4
Rhythm: Ballad or 8 Beat

Words and Music by
Andraé Crouch

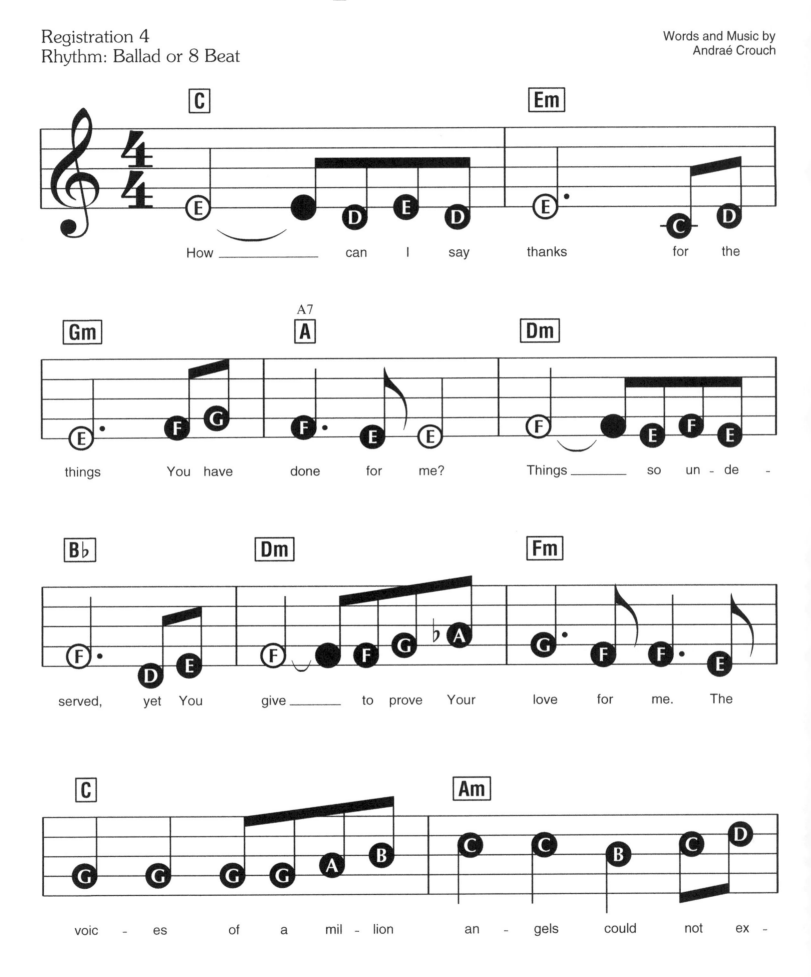

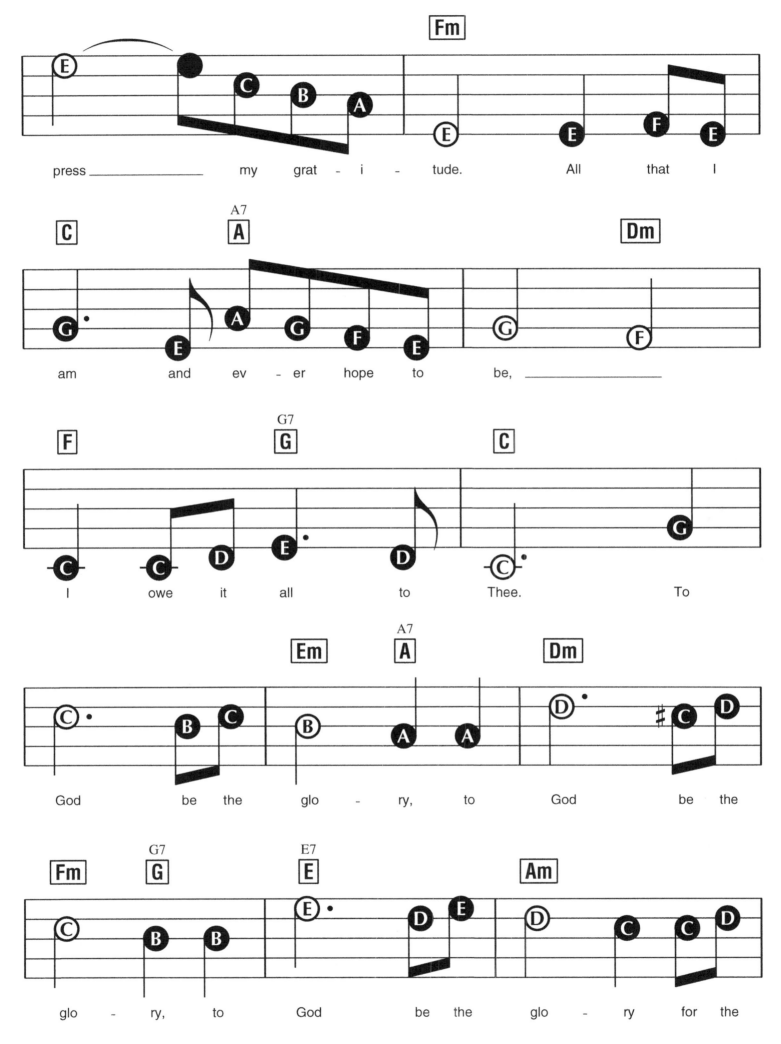

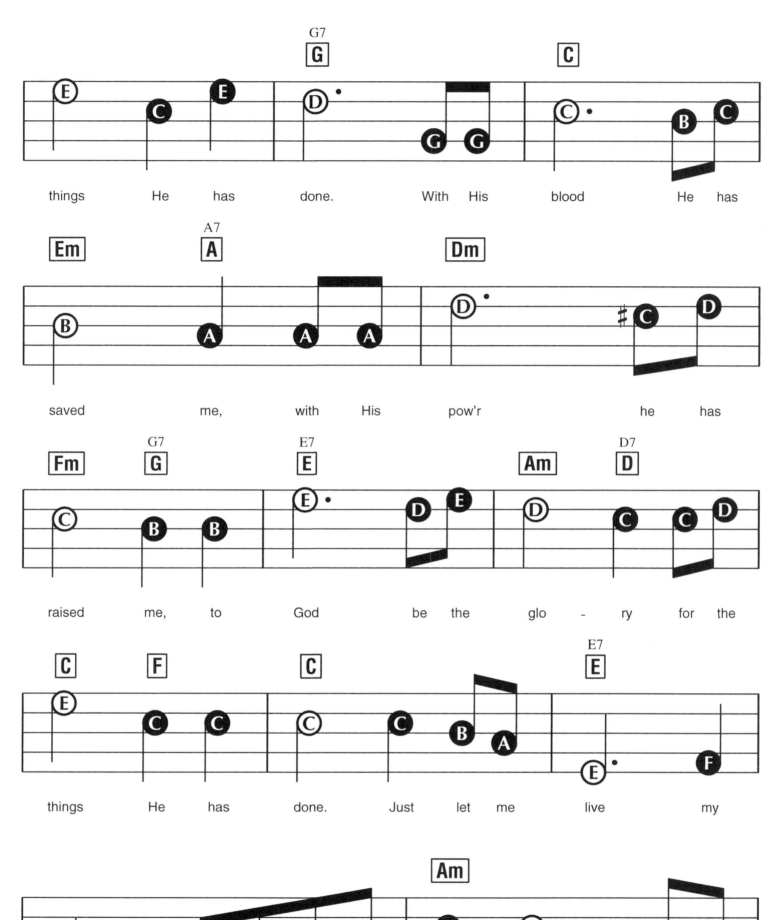

34

things He has done. With His blood He has

saved me, with His pow'r he has

raised me, to God be the glo - ry for the

things He has done. Just let me live my

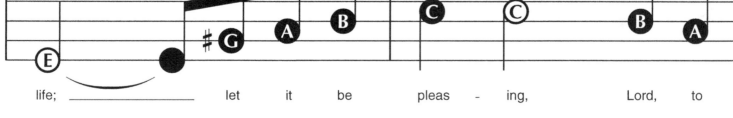

life; _____ let it be pleas - ing, Lord, to

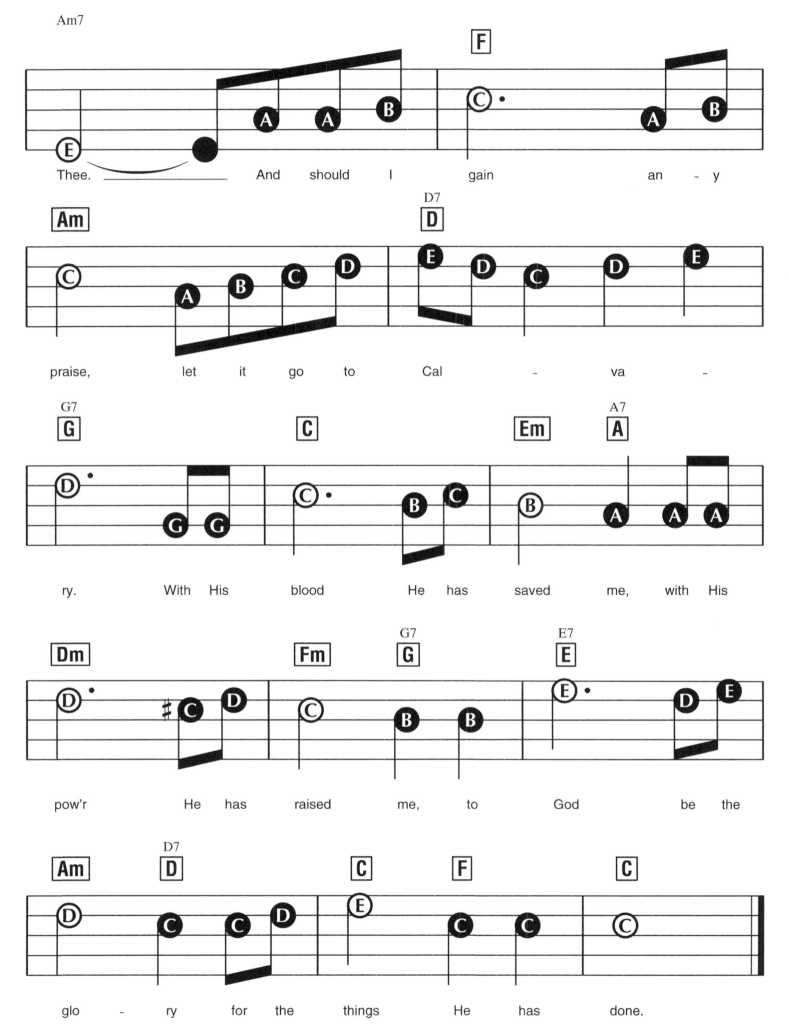

On the Jericho Road

Registration 7
Rhythm: Shuffle or Swing

Words and Music by
Don S. McCrossan

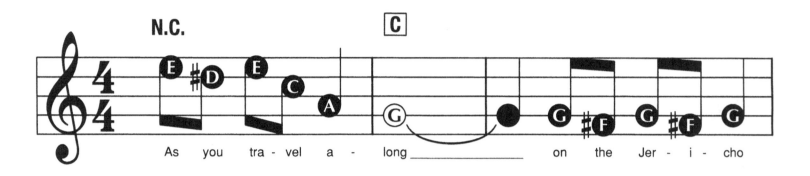

As you tra - vel a - long _____ on the Jer - i - cho

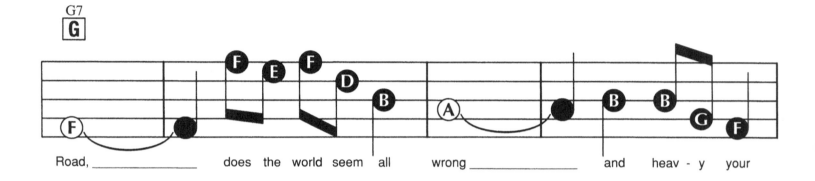

Road, _____ does the world seem all wrong _____ and heav - y your

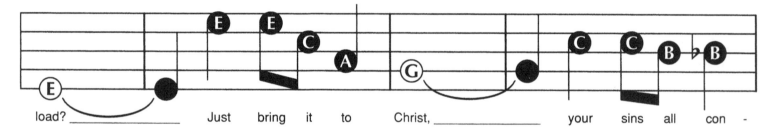

load? _____ Just bring it to Christ, _____ your sins all con -

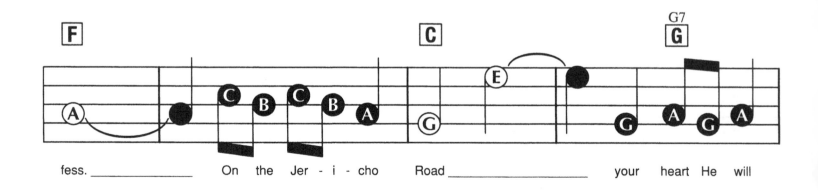

fess. _____ On the Jer - i - cho Road _____ your heart He will

(There'll Be)
Peace in the Valley
(For Me)

Registration 2
Rhythm: Waltz

Words and Music by
Thomas A. Dorsey

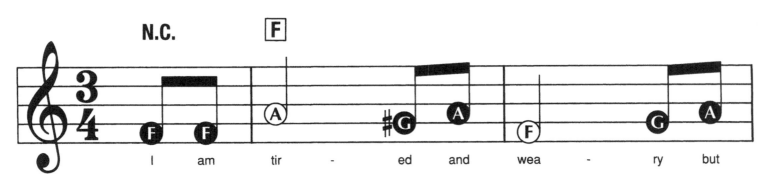

I am tir - ed and wea - ry but

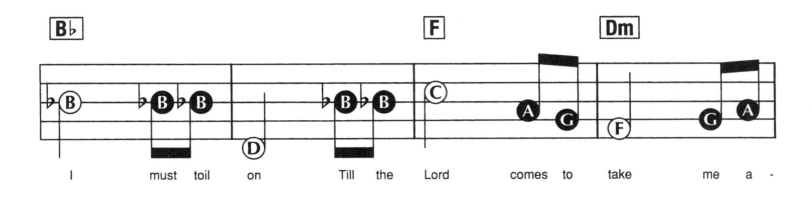

I must toil on Till the Lord comes to take me a -

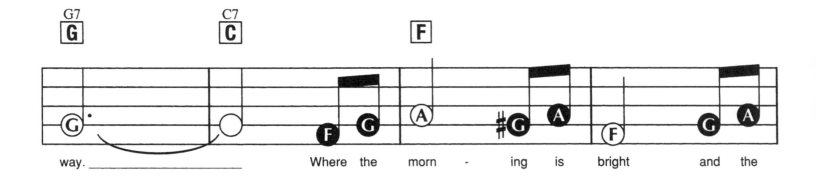

way. Where the morn - ing is bright and the

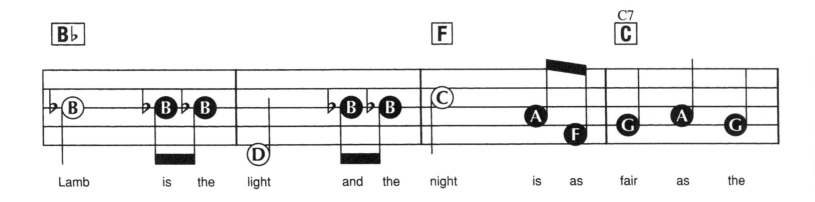

Lamb is the light and the night is as fair as the

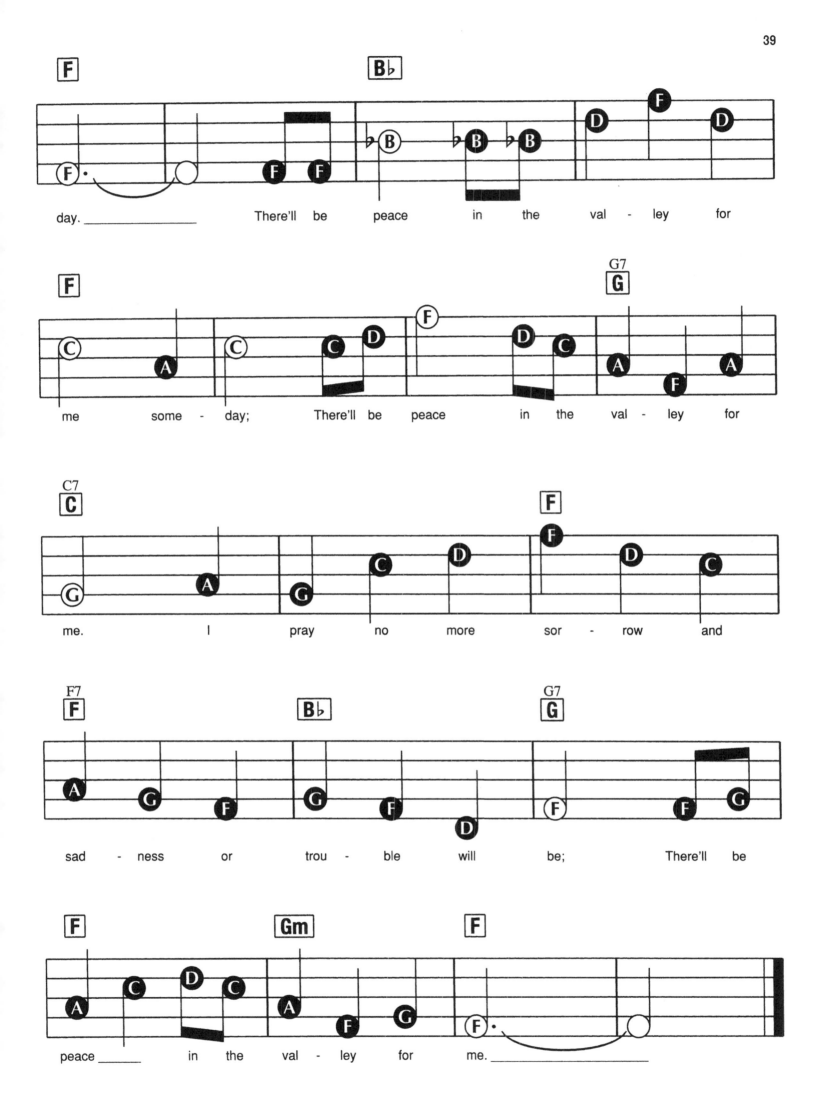

Precious Lord, Take My Hand
(Take My Hand, Precious Lord)

Registration 9
Rhythm: Waltz

Words and Music by
Thomas A. Dorsey

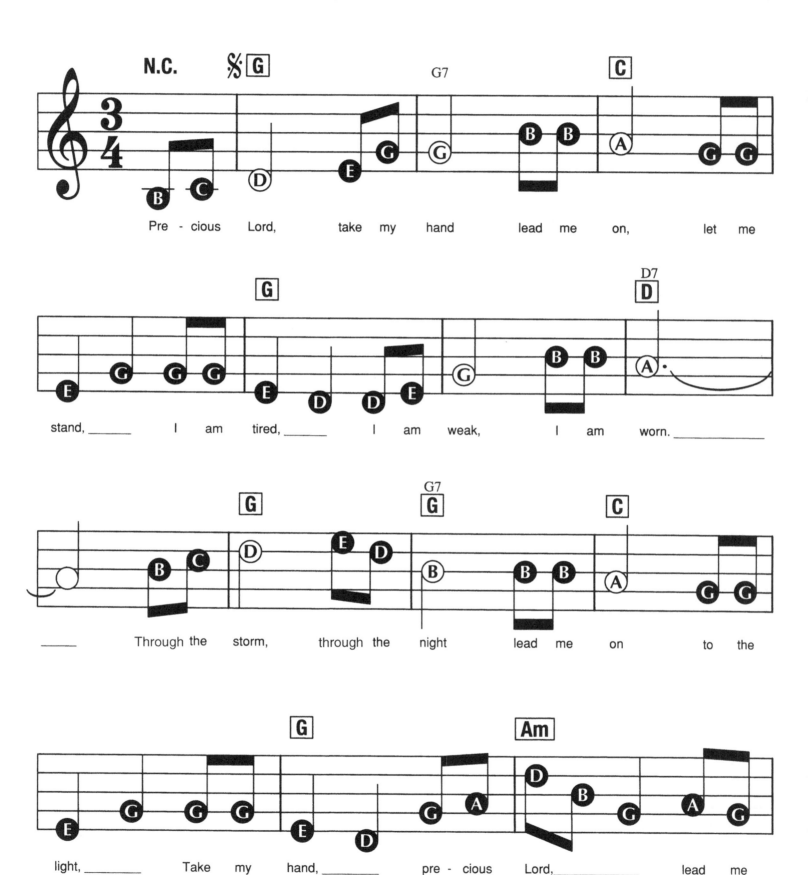

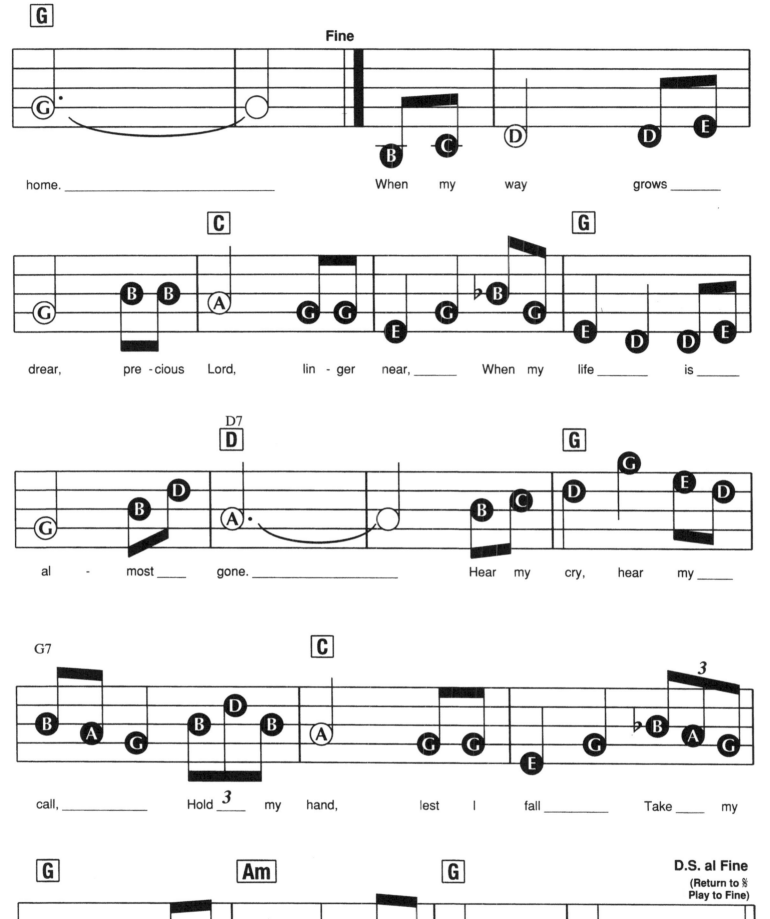

home. _____ When my way grows _____

drear, pre - cious Lord, lin - ger near, _____ When my life _____ is _____

al - most ____ gone. _____ Hear my cry, hear my ____

call, _____ Hold ____ my hand, lest I fall _____ Take ____ my

D.S. al Fine
(Return to 𝄋
Play to Fine)

hand, _____ pre - cious Lord, _____ lead me home. _____ Pre - cious

Put Your Hand in the Hand

Registration 8
Rhythm: Rock or Jazz Rock

Words and Music by
Gene MacLellan

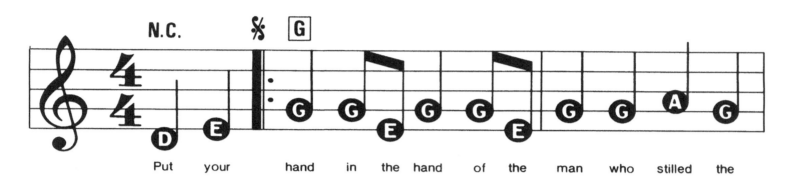

Put your hand in the hand of the man who stilled the

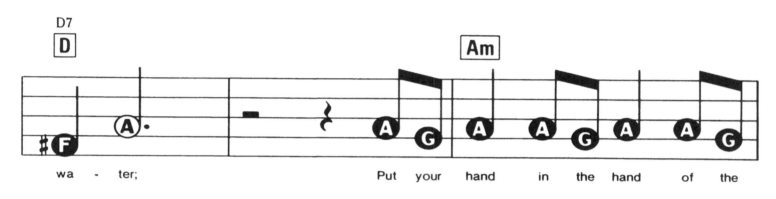

wa - ter; Put your hand in the hand of the

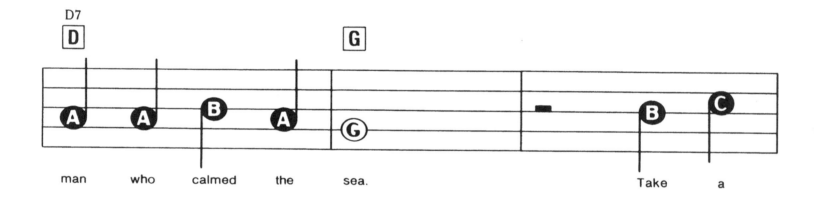

man who calmed the sea. Take a

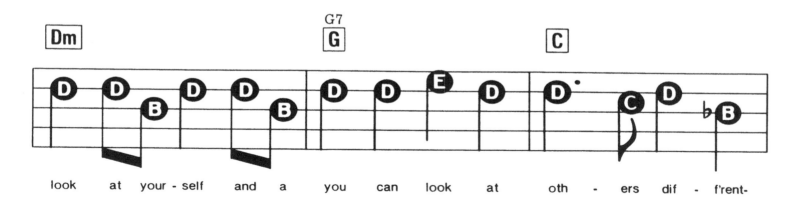

look at your - self and a you can look at oth - ers dif - f'rent-

44

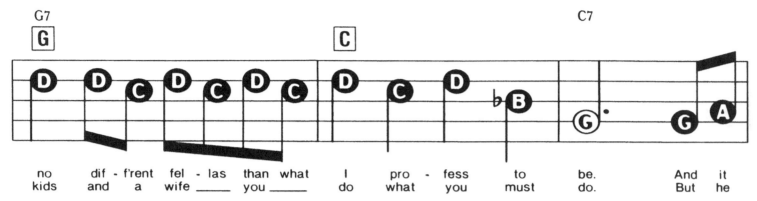

no dif-f'rent fel-las than what I pro-fess to be. And it
kids and a wife _____ you _____ do what you must do. But he

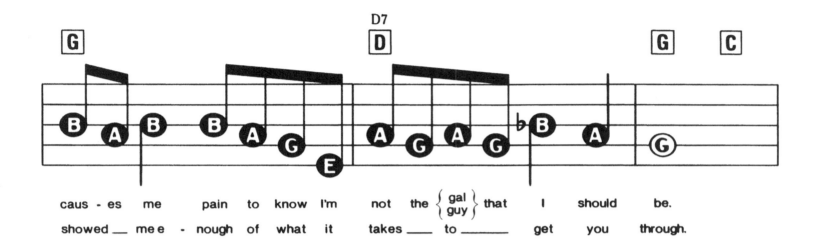

caus-es me pain to know I'm not the { gal / guy } that I should be.
showed _ me e-nough of what it takes _____ to _____ get you through.

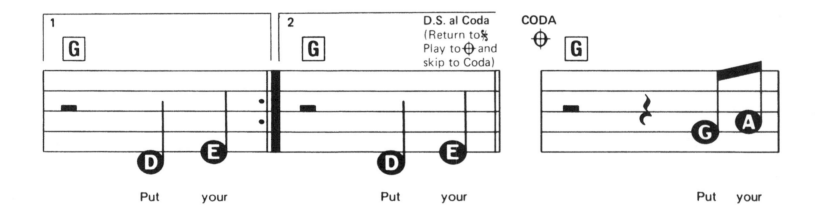

1
G

Put your

2
G

D.S. al Coda
(Return to 𝄋
Play to ⊕ and
skip to Coda)

Put your

CODA
⊕
G

Put your

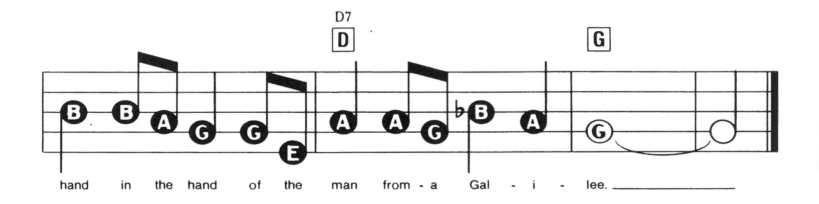

hand in the hand of the man from a Gal - i - lee. _____

Reach Out to Jesus

Registration 7
Rhythm: Waltz

Words and Music by
Ralph Carmichael

Is your bur - den heav - y as you bear it all a -
Is the life you're liv - ing filled with sor - row and de -

lone? _____ Does the road you trav - el har - bor
spair? _____ Does the fu - ture press you with its

dan - gers yet un - known? _____ Are you grow - ing
wor - ry and its care? _____ Are you tired and

wea - ry in the strug - gle of it all? _____
friend - less, have you al - most lost your way? _____

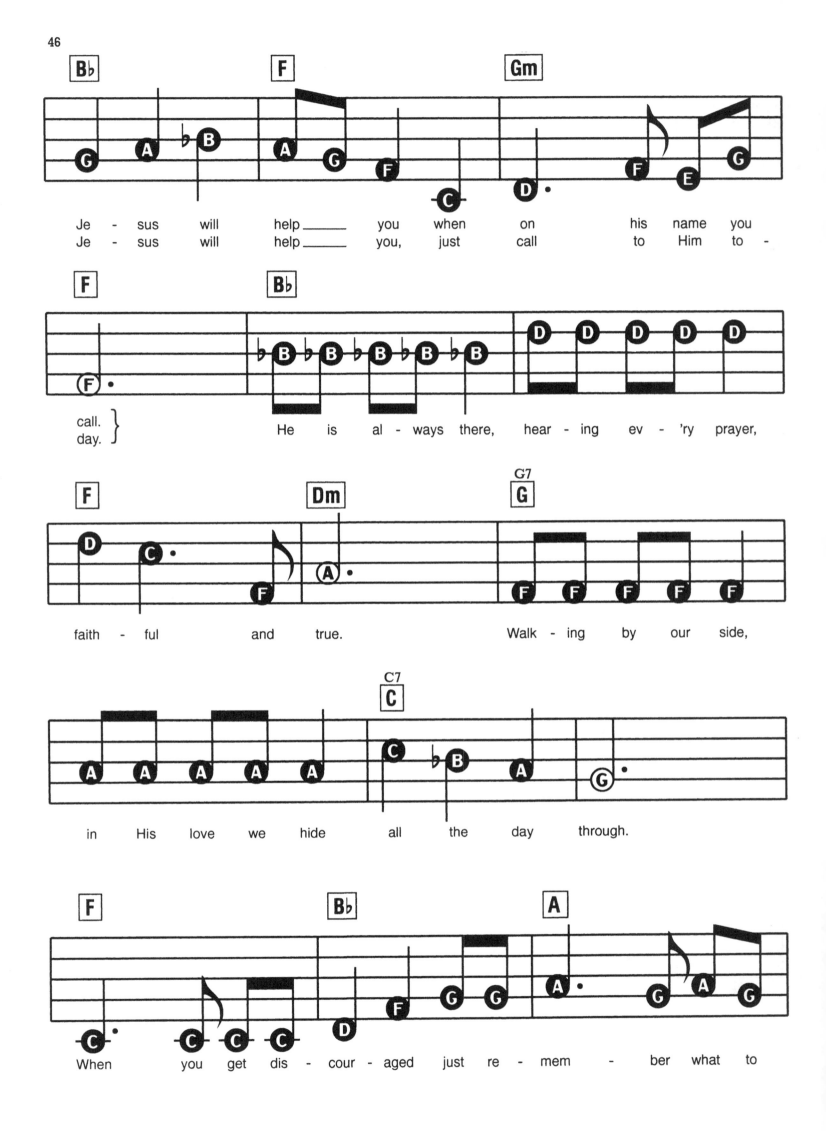

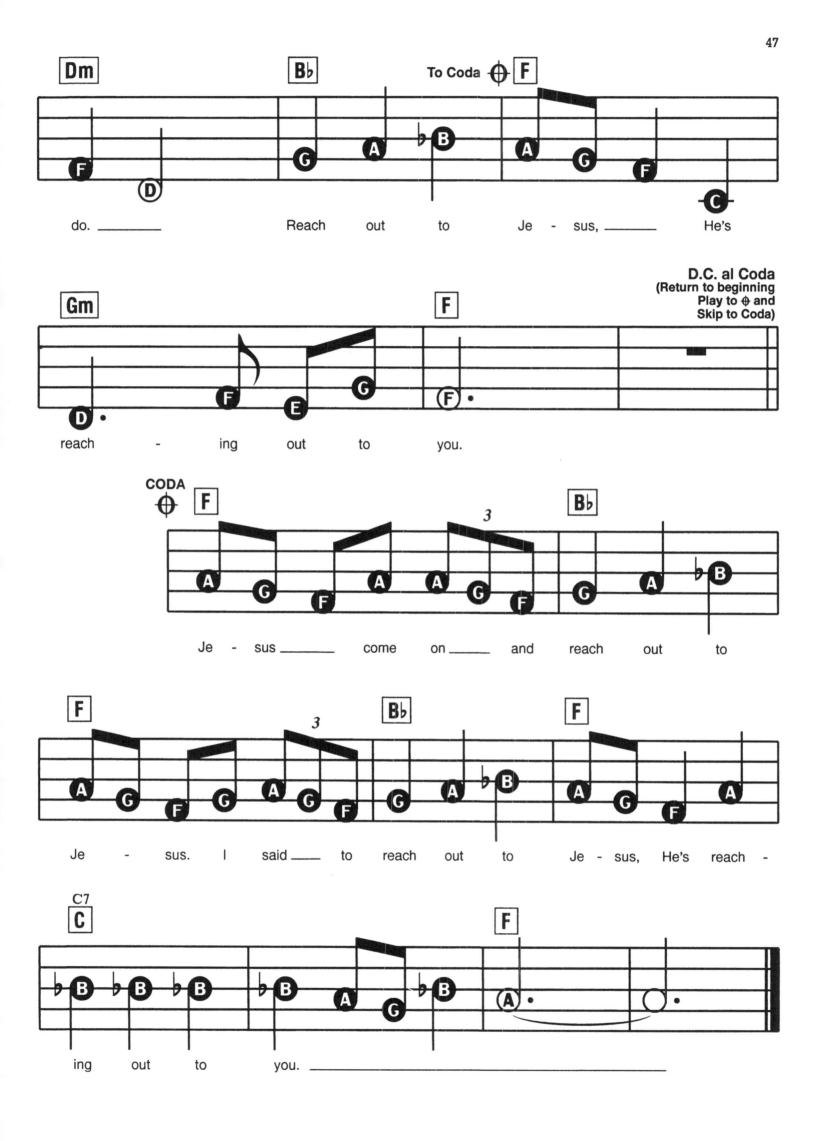

Ready to Go Home

Registration 9
Rhythm: Country or Fox Trot

Words and Music by
Hank Williams

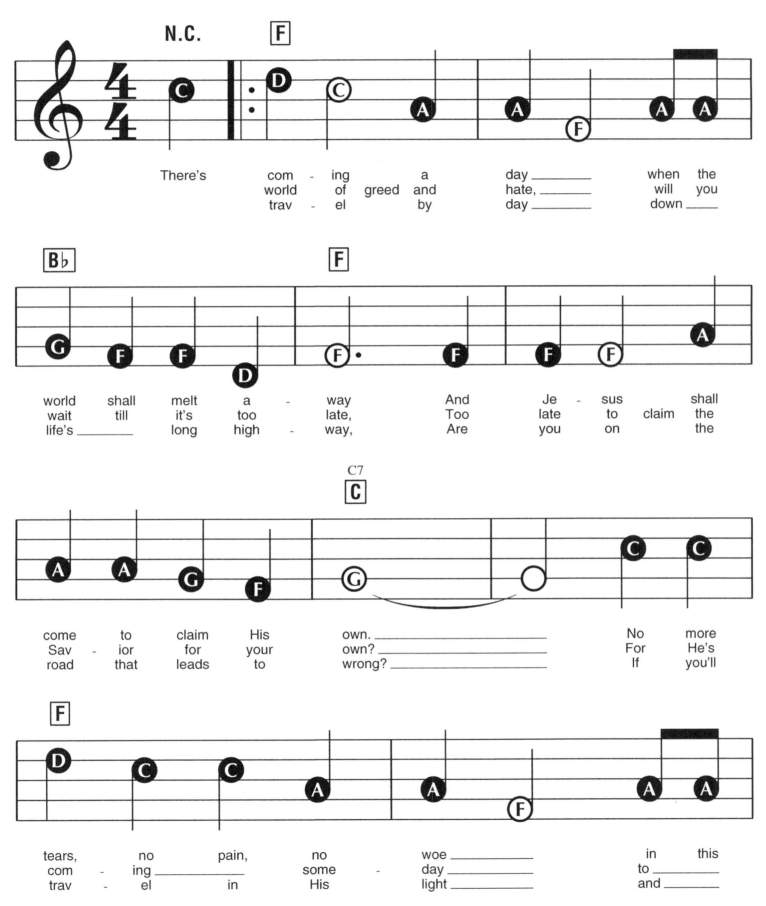

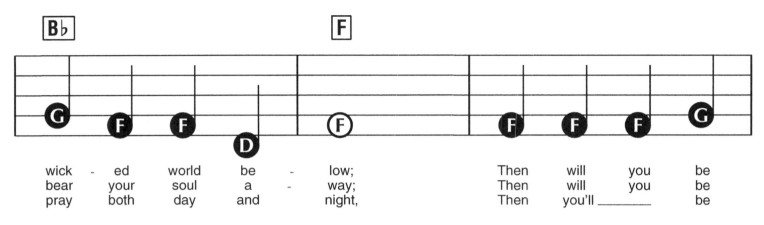

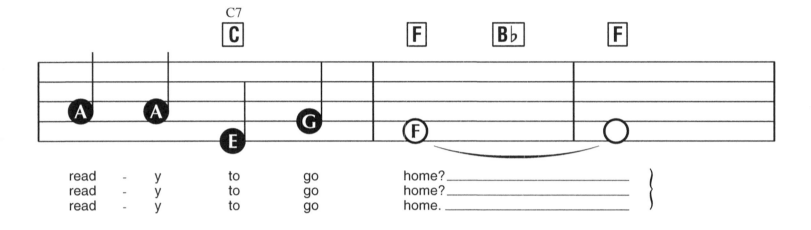

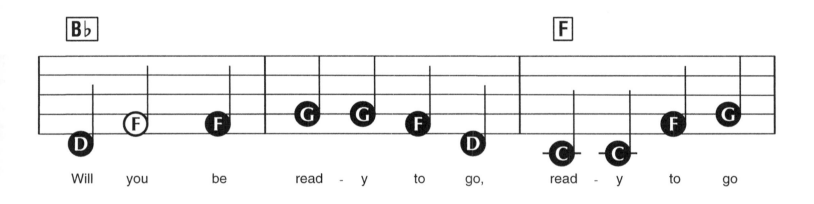

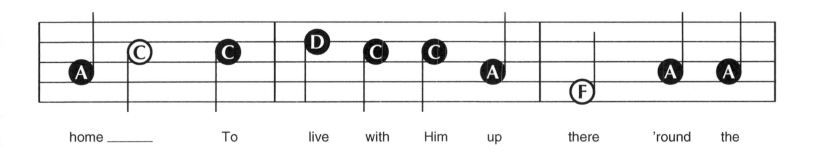

50

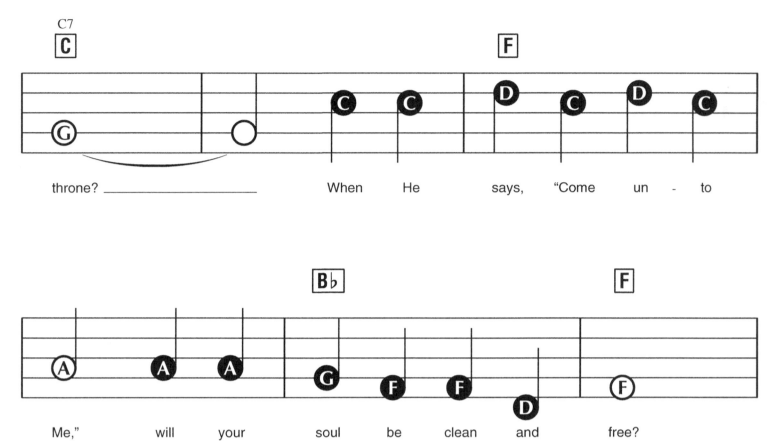

throne? _____ When He says, "Come un - to

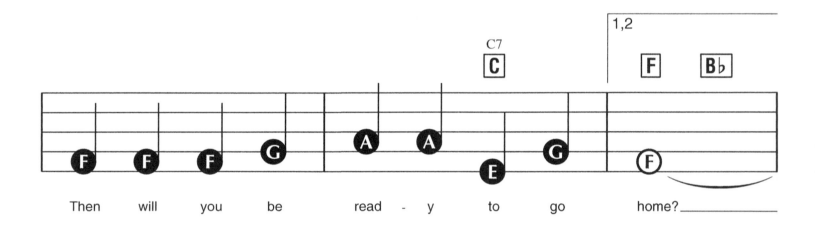

Me," will your soul be clean and free?

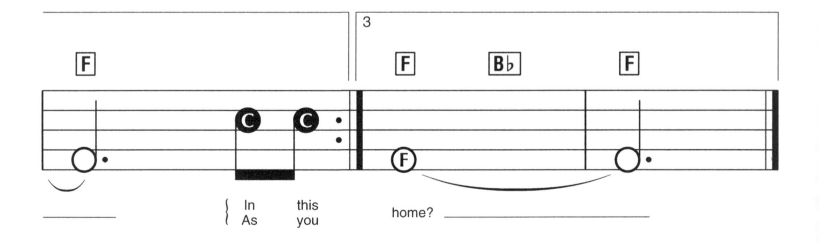

Then will you be read - y to go home?_____

F _____ In this / As you home? _____

Sheltered in the Arms of God

Registration 8
Rhythm: 4/4 Ballad or Fox Trot

Words and Music by Dottie Rambo
and Jimmie Davis

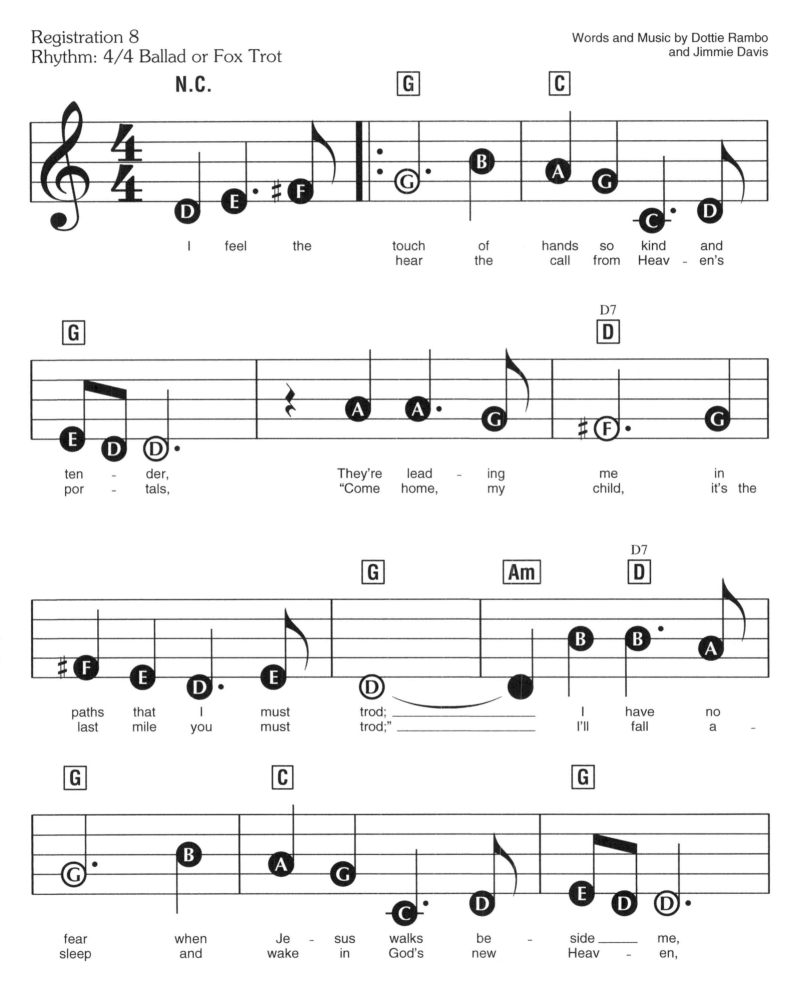

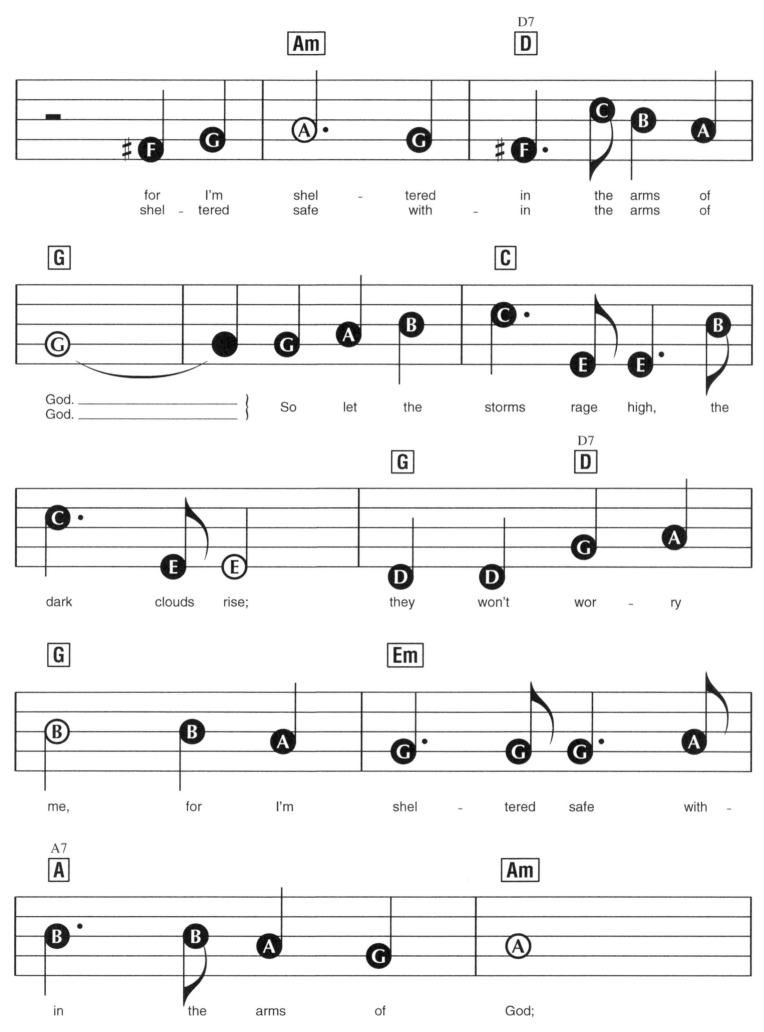

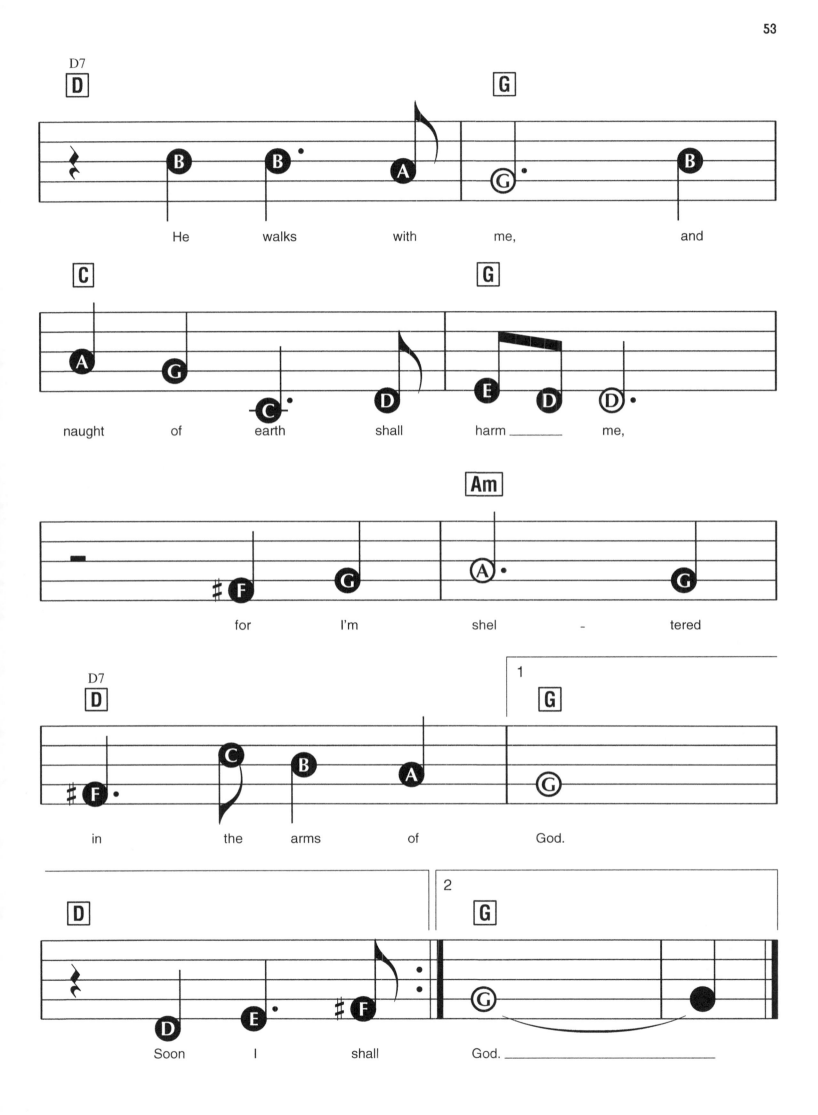

Soon and Very Soon

Registration 8
Rhythm: Soul or Fox Trot

Words and Music by
Andraé Crouch

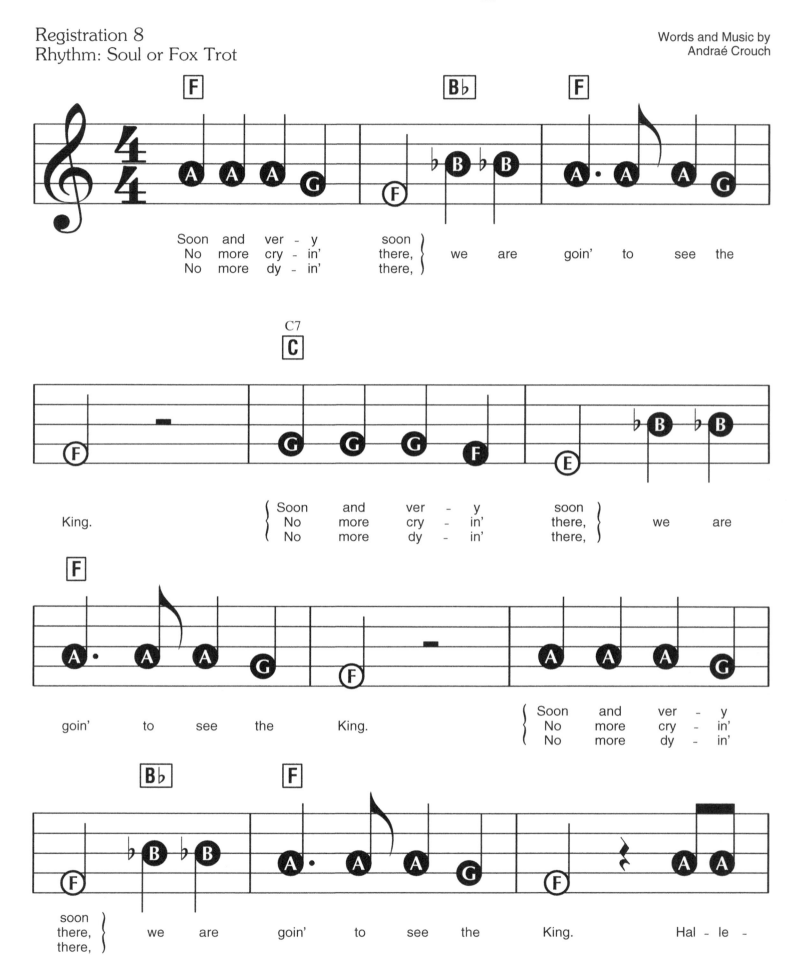

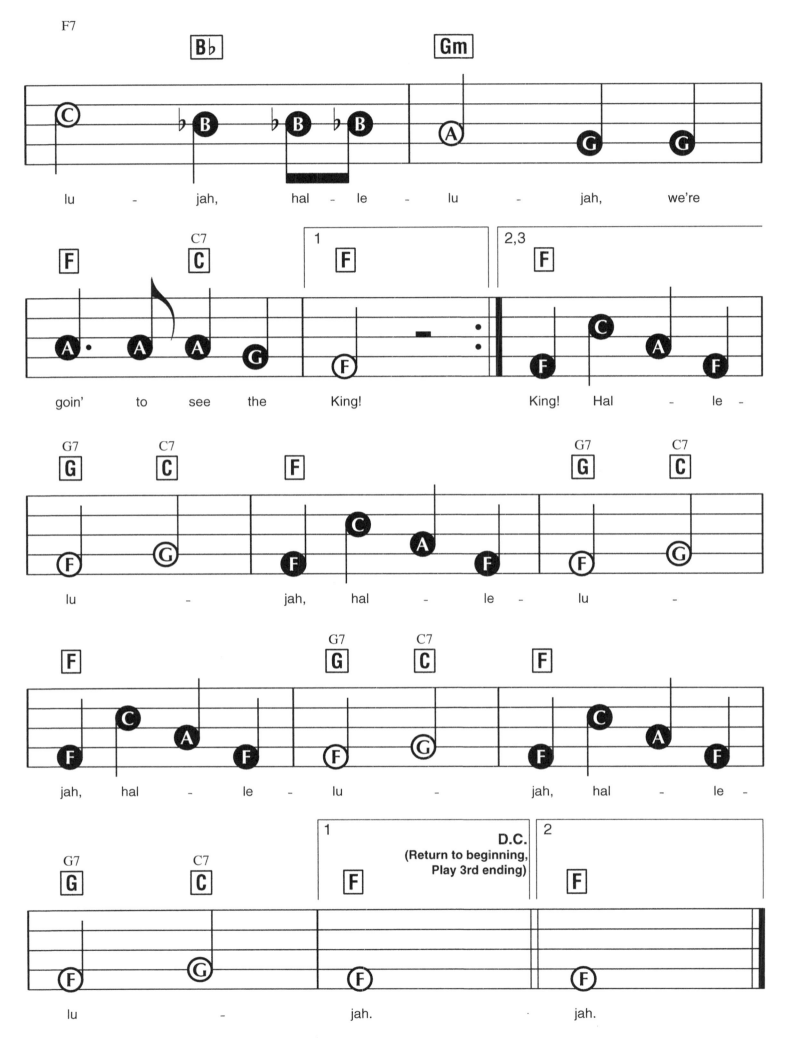

Suppertime

Registration 5
Rhythm: Swing

Words and Music by
Ira F. Stanphill

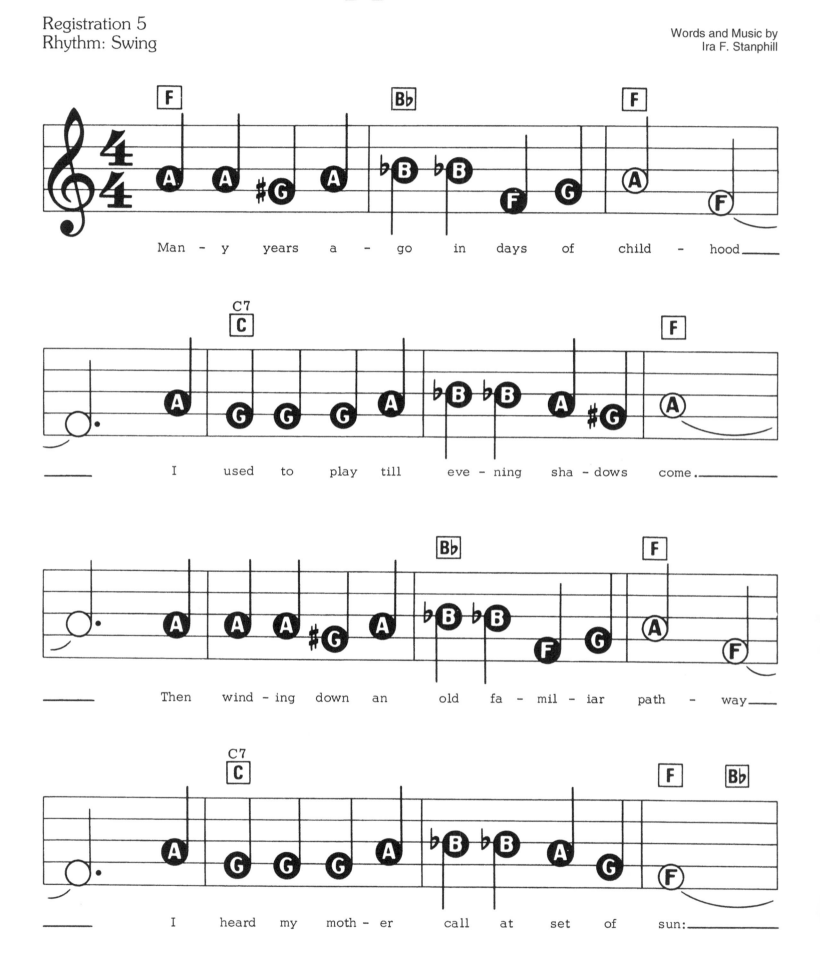

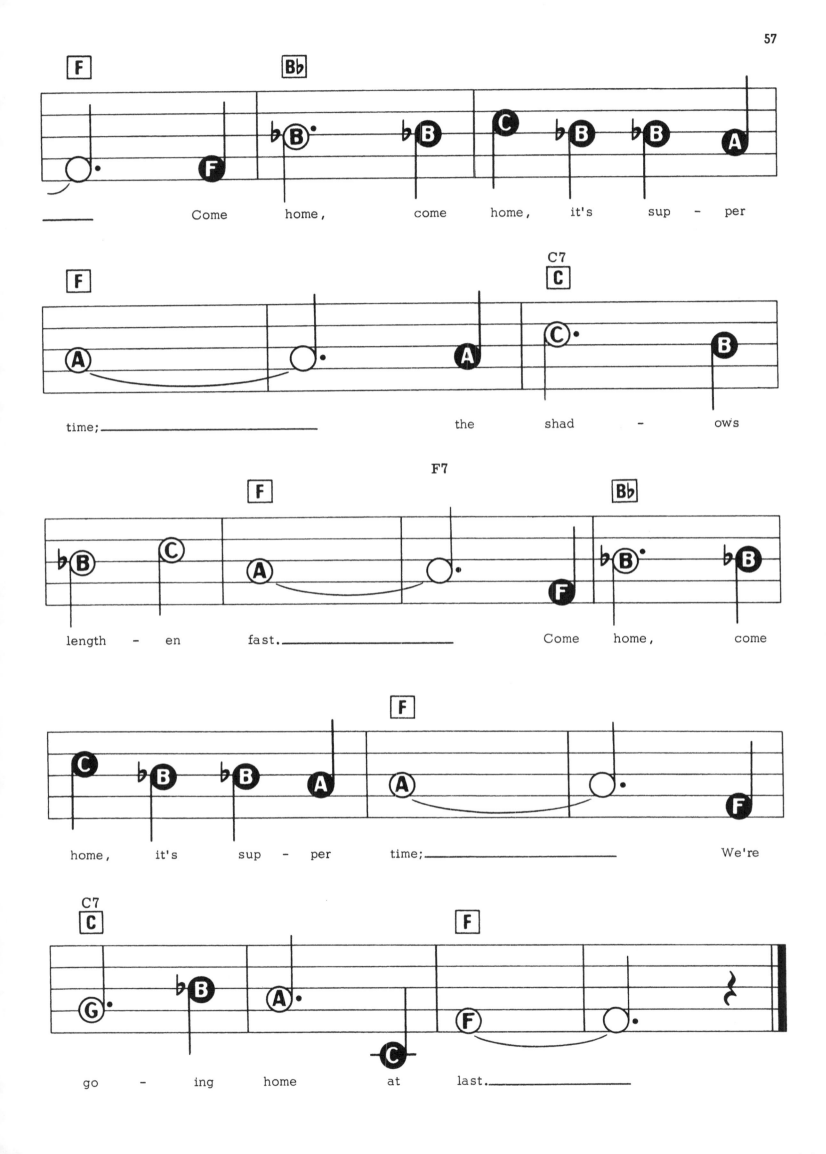

We Are So Blessed

Registration 3
Rhythm: Waltz

Words and Music by Greg Nelson,
Gloria and William J. Gaither

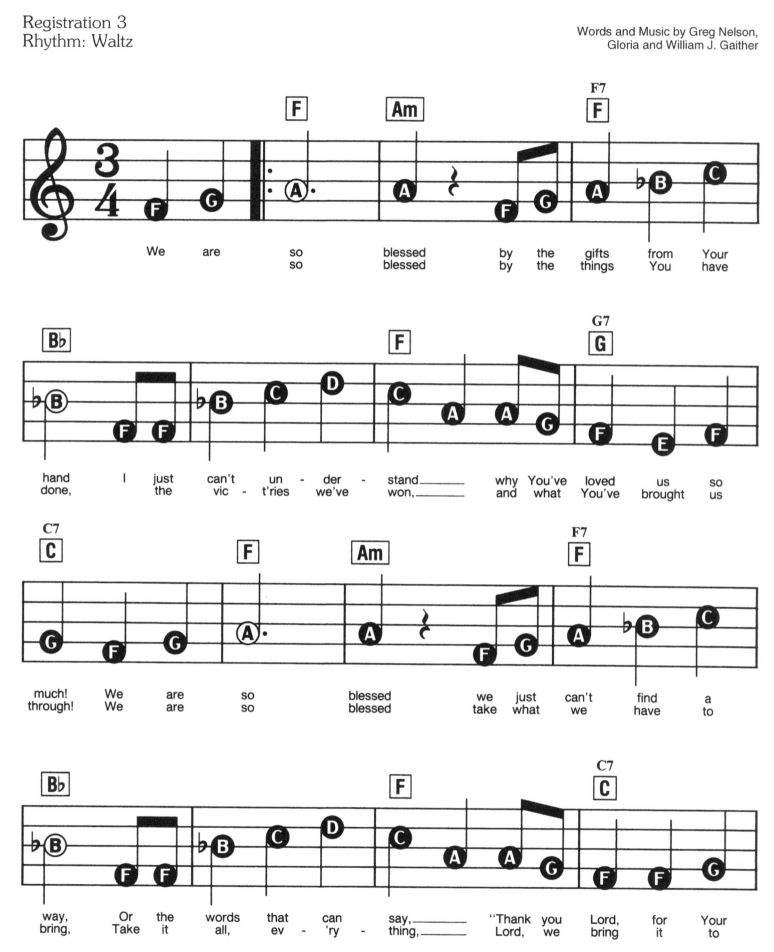

59

We Have Come into His House

Registration 1
Rhythm: Slow Rock or Shuffle

Words and Music by
Bruce Ballinger

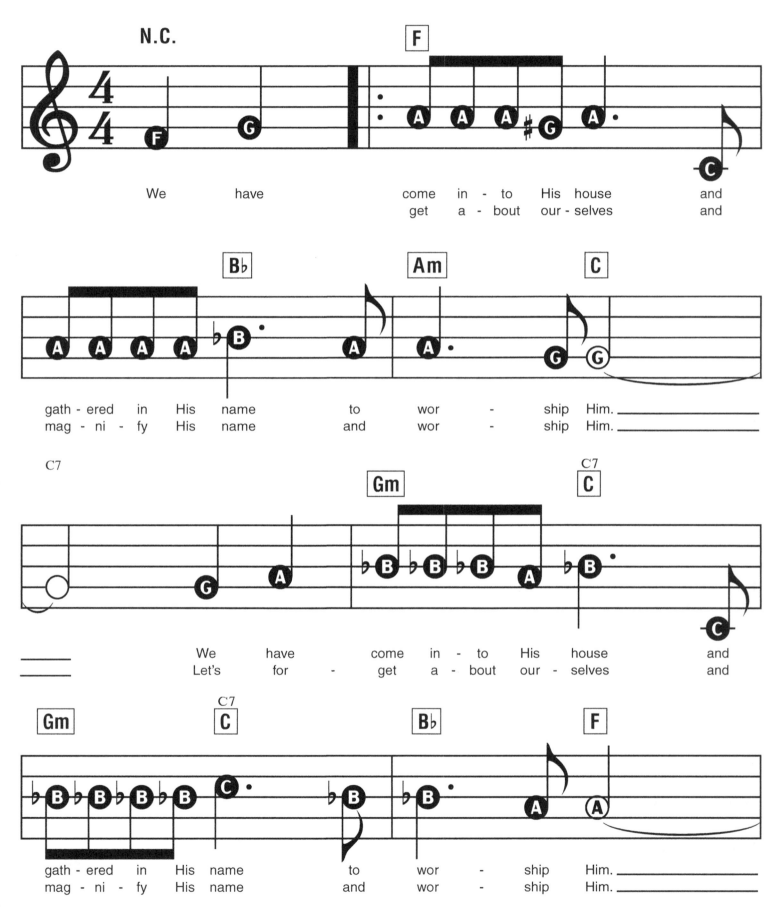

gath - ered in His name to wor - ship Him. _____
mag - ni - fy His name and wor - ship Him. _____

61

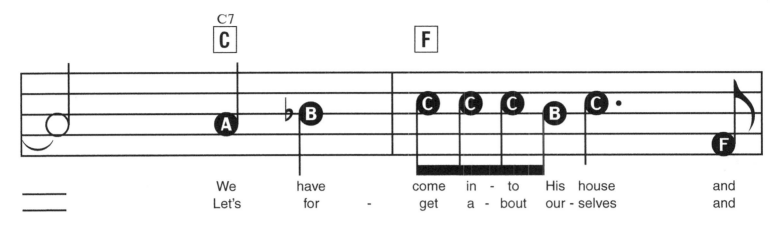

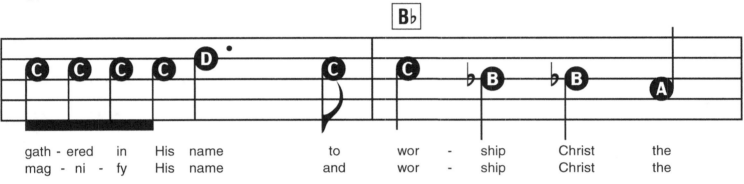

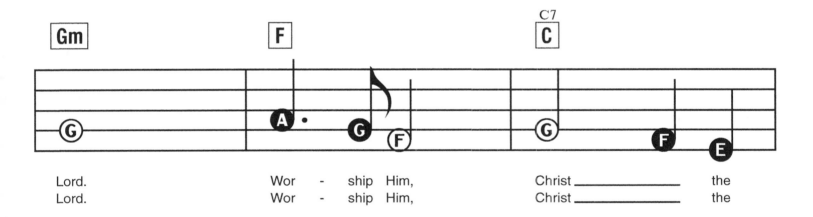

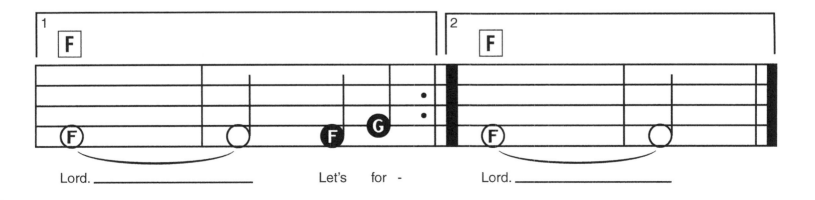

That's What Jesus Means to Me

Registration 3
Rhythm: Ballad or Slow Rock

Words and Music by
William J. Gaither

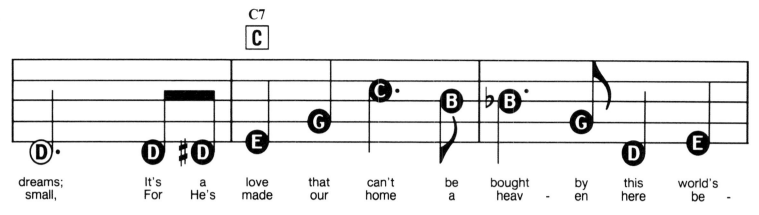

dreams; It's a love that can't be bought by this world's
small, For He's made our home a heav - en here be -

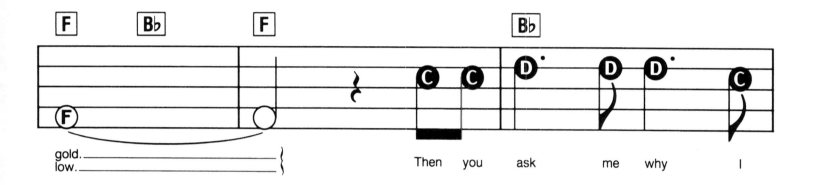

gold. _____
low. _____

Then you ask me why I

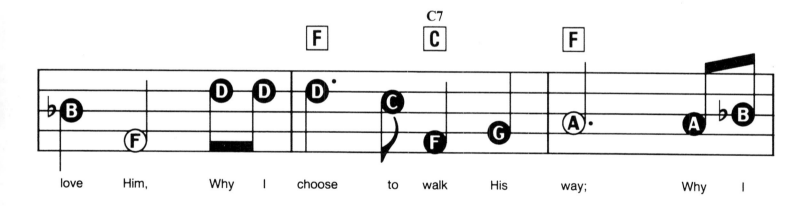

love Him, Why I choose to walk His way; Why I

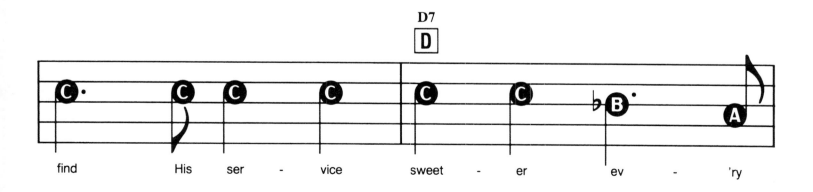

find His ser - vice sweet - er ev - 'ry

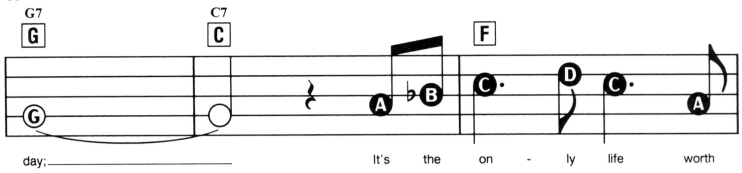

day;_____ It's the on - ly life worth

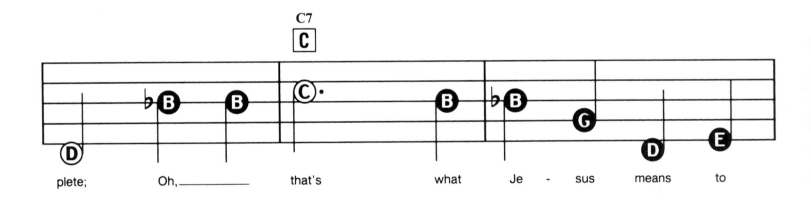

liv - ing He has made my world com -
(our home)

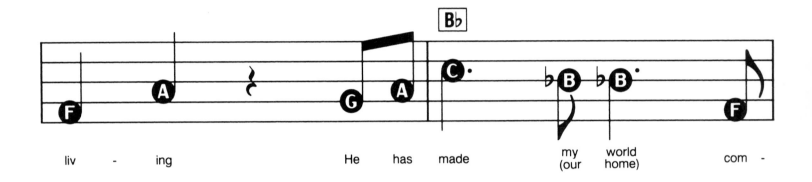

plete; Oh,_____ that's what Je - sus means to

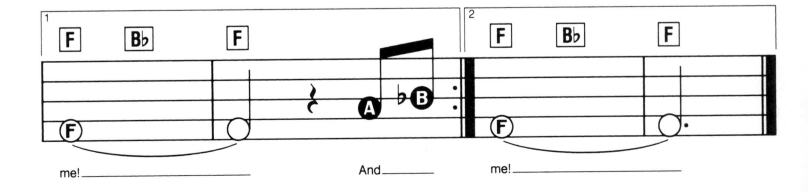

me!_____ And_____ me!_____